Making Artisan Chocolates

Making Artisan Chocolates

FLAVOR-INFUSED CHOCOLATES, TRUFFLES, AND CONFECTIONS

ANDREW GARRISON SHOTTS

Award-Winning Pastry Chef and Chocolatier

Photography by Madeline Polss

Foreword by Nick Malgieri

GLOUCESTER MASSACHUSETTS

QUARRY BOOKS

First published in the United States of America by
Quarry Books, a member of
Quayside Publishing Group
33 Commercial Street
Gloucester, Massachusetts 01930-5089
Telephone: (978) 282-9590
Fax: (978) 283-2742
www.rockpub.com

Andrew Garrison Shotts
Garrison Confections
815 Hope Street
Providence, RI 02906
401-490-2740
www.garrisonconfections.com

Library of Congress Cataloging-in-Publication Data
Shotts, Andrew Garrison.
    Making artisan chocolates : flavor-infused chocolates, truffles, and confections /
Andrew Garrison Shotts ; photography by Madeline Polss.
        p.   cm.
    Includes index.
    ISBN 1-59253-310-8 (pbk.)
    1. Chocolate candy. I. Title.

    TX791.S52 2007
    641.8'53—dc22   2006019247
                                                     CIP

10 9 8 7 6 5 4 3 2

ISBN-13: 978-1-59253-310-7
ISBN-10: 1-59253-310-8

Special thanks to Tina Wright for her editorial consulation.

Design and Layout: Peter M. Blaiwas, Vern Associates, Inc.
Cover Design: Howard Grossman
Photography: Madeline Polss

Printed in Singapore

DEDICATION

This book is dedicated to the memory of my parents. My mother, Sue, first instilled in me my love of cooking. She would call me from work and walk me through simple preparations to help get dinner started before she arrived home. I can still hear her telling me to pour "two bloops of oil in the pan." From my father, Don, I learned work ethic and discipline. He taught me that a worthwhile outcome is fully dependent on the time and effort it takes to get there. I am thankful for their love and wisdom in pointing me in the right direction time and time again. I honor their memories every day when I go to work and do what I love.

CONTENTS

FOREWORD

By Nick Malgieri

With close to thirty years' experience teaching and writing about chocolate, desserts, and baking, I've seen many a trend come and go. My greatest pleasure has been to witness a younger generation of pastry chefs and chocolatiers grow up around me, winning awards and recognition for their fine work. Andrew Shotts is at the front of that group, whose dedication to their craft and disciplined hard work have helped them gain significant recognition at a young age. His resumé includes extensive work experience in Italy and France, head pastry chef positions in such renowned establishments as La Côte Basque and the Russian Tea Room, and four years as the corporate pastry chef for Guittard Chocolate Company. His first business venture in New York, the Chocolate Loft, combined a teaching kitchen and a production facility for preparing his first line of chocolates. While there, he attracted students and teachers from all over the world, and quickly developed a reputation for being as gifted a teacher as he is a chocolatier.

Andrew loves to shares his knowledge of chocolate and its complexities. He is as clear and gifted a writer as he is a master of developing creative and unusual flavoring components for his confections. In his book you'll find precise step-by-step instructions for all the basic chocolate processes, as well as charts, techniques, and hints to help you strike out on your own to and pursue your own creative impulses. Like every great teacher, Andrew gives you the basics *and* encourages your own creativity.

If you haven't been fortunate enough to receive a gift of Andrew's Garrison Confections, or to attend one of his classes, *Making Artisan Chocolates* will give you both—you'll feel as though he's right beside you, teaching you how to create these luscious chocolate treats that are as much fun to prepare as they are to taste. I can't think of anyone else who could do that better than Andrew Shotts.

Nick Malgieri is the award-winning author of several highly-acclaimed cookbooks, including How to Bake, Chocolate, *and* A Baker's Tour. *He also serves as Director of Baking Programs at the Institute of Culinary Education in New York City.*

INTRODUCTION

In the world of artisan chocolates, my company, Garrison Confections, is known for creating new flavor combinations five times a year. We change our chocolate collections seasonally, based on the lunar calendar. Each collection comprises twelve bonbons, is named after the season in which it falls (Vernal Equinox, Summer Solstice, Autumnal Equinox, and Winter Solstice), and is only available during that specific season. Additionally, we create a new Valentine's Day collection each year called the Legendary Lovers Collection, also made up of twelve pieces.

Although it is quite a challenge to create sixty new flavors a year, I believe it is important to continually offer something new and interesting. This keeps us on our toes and allows us to take advantage of flavor trends.

I do not have one specific formula for creating new flavor fusions. At Garrison Confections, the creation of each new collection is a group effort. Throughout the year our store keeps track of customer requests and feedback. Many culinary students come through my kitchen every year; their minds are open to new ideas and they are not afraid to propose new flavors. And my kitchen staff keeps an ongoing list of ideas culled from research, conversations, or, if we are on deadline, pulled out of thin air.

A few of our bestsellers have come from adaptations of past desserts I created when I was a pastry chef in New York City. The peppered pineapple chocolate in chapter seven is a reinvention of a thinly sliced fresh pineapple carpaccio with fresh lime juice and a dusting of black pepper, whereas the strawberry-balsamic piece was originally a garnish for ice cream. I created the fennel chocolate featured in chapter six several seasons ago. The inspiration for this concoction came while having dinner at a favorite Providence restaurant, Chez Pascal. And our neighbor Carol is responsible for the spiced nut praline I recently created.

My point is this: Inspiration is everywhere as long as you are open to seeking it out.

To be able to translate inspiration to finished product, however, you must first understand the basic techniques of working with chocolate. One of the biggest misconceptions I come across is the idea that chocolate bonbons and candies are made by simply melting and then refrigerating the molded or coated pieces to help the chocolate set. This is a quick and easy short-term fix to help chocolate harden, but not the proper way to make chocolate confections.

To really become proficient at working with chocolate, and to eventually be able to invent your own fabulous creations, you will need to have a good working knowledge of the chocolate-tempering process. In writing this book I have tried to take information that can be somewhat confusing and make it less so. If you only truly read one section of this book, please pay attention to chapter two. Mastering the techniques in that chapter will give you a good foundation on which to build future chocolate skills.

Chapter three teaches you how to create different flavor combinations and how to experiment on your own. As you become proficient at making artisan chocolates, you will want to show off your skills to friends and family; chapter four provides fun ideas on pairings and presentations. Wine and chocolate parties are a great reason to invite everyone over to sample your efforts. When paired correctly, wine and chocolate enhance and bring out each other's subtle nuances. And you are sure to become everyone's favorite dinner guest when you show up with a hostess gift of chocolates artfully wrapped and creatively presented.

After mastering the basics, part two shows you how to put the techniques into practice, with forty recipes with which to experiment. Use these recipes as a guide to making your own unique flavor fusions. I hope they will give you a sense of how to pair flavors, both complementary and contrasting, as well as textures.

I love to make chocolate and I think it shows in all the products I create. If you enjoy the process of thinking about flavor combinations and putting them together to create chocolates and confections, then I am sure you will come up with some winners of your own. And remember that, while it may take time and practice to master the art of making chocolate, it will be time and effort well spent. So get ready to have fun and be creative!

Counter clockwise from left to right: Classic Dark 72 percent, page 86; Banana Caramel, page 100; Lemongrass-Coconut, page 93.

TIP:

I recommend that even the most experienced cooks take the time to read the Recipe Notes on page 50, as chocolate-making techniques vary from traditional baking methods.

Part One

THE BASICS

Just as a house cannot be built without a good foundation, a recipe cannot yield a good result without some essential components. This section will walk you through the bare bones of what you will need to create the chocolates in this book. After reviewing the basics of chocolate-making ingredients and the importance of using only the best you can find, you will learn how to temper chocolate—the most important cooking technique you will need in order to master the recipes in this book. Although it may be difficult at first, tempering chocolate is simply a matter of practice and patience. Pay attention to each step and remember what the chocolate looks like as it goes through each stage. Once you have a visual memory of what to watch for, the process will come more naturally.

After you have assembled all your ingredients and have a good understanding of how to temper chocolate, all that is left to do is create fabulous flavor fusions. This is the fun part, as you are limited only by your imagination. Just remember that creating flavor combinations—good ones that is—is really a matter of common sense and balance. Don't try to mix flavors that seem completely opposite just for the sake of creating something different. Stop and think about how certain flavors might mix together. And once you have decided to create your own combinations, follow the "less is more" theory, at least for your first few attempts.

Chapter One

Selecting Ingredients

The most important aspect of creating great chocolates is using quality ingredients. Although techniques take time and effort to learn, quality ingredients are plentiful and generally easy to find. Quality chocolate is the backbone of your confections, so understanding its origins and current options is an important first step to making artisan chocolates. If you start with great chocolate and add the best of any other ingredient that you can find and afford, half the challenge is already won.

A Very Brief History Lesson

Since before its discovery in the New World in 1502 by Christopher Columbus, and then its introduction to the Spanish courts in 1528 by Hernán Cortés, chocolate has been one of the world's greatest epicurean delicacies.

Prized by the ancient Mayans and Aztecs for its aphrodisiac and energizing qualities, chocolate, in the form of crushed cocoa beans derived from the seeds of the cacao tree, was originally consumed as a beverage. The Spanish promptly added sugar to make the chocolate more palatable, planted cacao trees throughout their colonies, and kept their find a secret from the rest of Europe for the next one hundred years.

By the mid-1600s, drinkable chocolate was widely available throughout Europe, though it was still considered a luxury and consumed mostly by the upper classes. Recognizing chocolate's financial potential, other countries soon followed Spain's agricultural lead and cacao plantations quickly sprang up in Sri Lanka, the West Indies, Venezuela, Sumatra, and Java. Chocolate made its way back across the ocean with the settlers relocating to the colonies, and in 1765 the first chocolate factory in colonial America opened its doors.

The 1800s was a great century for chocolate innovation: Cocoa powder was developed, the preferred form of chocolate consumption went from liquid to solid, the Swiss added dried milk to the recipe to create milk chocolate, the Industrial Revolution brought chocolate to the masses, and Milton Hershey founded the Hershey Chocolate Company. But chocolate as we think of it today really evolved in the twentieth century. Most of the candy bars we, our parents, and our grandparents grew up with were invented within the last one hundred years. Filled chocolates, first produced in Switzerland in the early part of the century, owe their present popularity to a handful of higher-end chocolate companies and their marketing message of chocolate as the affordable luxury.

During the past decade, a new sector has been created within the chocolate industry: handmade artisan chocolates. As pastry chefs have become chocolatiers, bringing their artistic abilities to the art of making chocolate, the entire look and feel of luxury chocolates has changed. Classic flavor combinations have given way to unusual and daring ones, and spices and herbs, once relegated to savory cooking, are now found in chocolate. Pastry chefs have also influenced the look of chocolate. Their design capabilities, combined with the computer technology that allows chocolatiers to create colorful, intricate designs, patterns, and logos on individual pieces of chocolate, have resulted in chocolate that looks as extraordinary as it tastes.

Chocolate, From Bean to Bar

Believe it or not, your favorite candy bar started out as a fruit. More specifically, it began as a cocoa pod, the fruit of the cacao tree. Cultivated only in countries located within 20 degrees north or south of the equator, *Theobroma cacao* is a tropical plant that thrives in rainy climates. Because it needs protection from the sun and wind, the cacao tree is generally planted under a canopy of leafy, taller trees such as banana trees and stands between 15 and

COCOA BEAN PLANTATIONS

All of the world's chocolate begins with only three different varieties of cocoa beans: *Criollo, Forastero,* and *Trinitario.* Where a cocoa-producing country is located relative to the equator dictates what type of bean will grow in that climate. Most of the modern cocoa plantations cultivate the Forastero bean, which accounts for approximately 70 percent of the worldwide production. These plantations can be found on the continent of Africa—in Ghana, the Ivory Coast, and Nigeria; in Central and Latin America—in Brazil, Colombia, Venezuela, Ecuador, and Costa Rica; and in the Dominican Republic. The Criollo bean, which accounts for only about 10 percent of worldwide production, can also be found in Colombia and Venezuela, as well as in Mexico, Nicaragua, and halfway around the world in Madagascar. The Trinitario bean, native to Trinidad and a hybrid of the Forastero and Criollo, makes up the difference in production and is grown in many of the same countries as the Criollo.

25 feet (4.6 and 7.6 m) tall at maturity. The oval pods that become the cocoa bean start off as pink and white flowers that grow from the branches of the tree. A mature tree is covered in thousands of flowers, but only about 10 percent of these will develop into mature fruit for harvesting.

Harvesting

Nearly all of the world's cocoa supply is grown on small family farms and harvested by hand. Pods ripen throughout the year, allowing for a continuous growing cycle. Experienced farmers select the cacao pods that are ready for harvesting and cut them away from the tree, using a machete or a long pole knife. Machetes are also used to prune the trees, keeping them healthy and productive and reducing the need for pesticides. After harvesting, the pods are split open. Mature pods contain forty to fifty light yellow seeds.

Fermentation

The seeds, contained in a gelatinous, sugary pulp, are removed from the pod, placed in wooden crates, covered with banana leaves or other leafy greens specific to the region, and allowed to ferment for up to five days. During fermentation, the flavor of the seeds begins to develop, the bitterness subsides, and the seeds become a rich brown color. The cacao seeds are now referred to as cocoa beans.

Drying

The process of drying the cocoa beans takes place either on the farm or at a processing plant. The fermented beans are spread out onto mats and turned frequently during the next five to seven days. The dried cocoa beans, now known as raw cocoa, are bagged, taken to market, and shipped to manufacturers worldwide.

Destoning and Cleaning

Upon arrival at its specific factory, the raw cocoa is inspected and tested for bacteria and other noncocoa particles. It is then cleaned and blended to create specific flavor characteristics before going into the roaster.

Roasting

Roasting, a crucial part of chocolate making, takes place in large rotating cylinders. Chocolate manufacturers vary on how long they roast their beans. Some roast at a lower temperature for a longer amount of time, while others use higher temperatures for a shorter time. Generally speaking, roasting can take between thirty minutes and two hours. Carefully controlled heat turns the beans a deep brown color and allows the characteristic chocolate aroma to develop. After roasting, the raw cocoa goes to the cracker and fanner. Using high force, the cracker throws the beans against the inside wall of the machine to crack off the shell. A fan then blows the bean one way and the shell, or husk, another. The husks are no longer needed for chocolate production and are either thrown out or sold to farmers for compost. The cracked beans are now called cocoa nibs.

Cocoa beans from pod

Nib Roasting

Like many of the steps that go into manufacturing chocolate, each company roasts their nibs differently. Cocoa nibs can be roasted with or without their shells. The process of roasting nibs without their shells is known as nib roasting. This process is not ideal because the bean particles are often not the same size, so smaller particles burn before the rest of the batch is fully roasted, and may give off a burnt flavor to the chocolate.

Grinding

A series of heavy steel rollers or grinding stones crush and liquefy the cocoa nibs into a shiny brown liquid called chocolate liquor (even though it does not contain any alcohol). At this point the chocolate liquor is either made into cocoa powder or turned into eating chocolate.

Cocoa Powder

Cocoa powder is created when chocolate liquor is pumped into giant hydraulic presses whose intense pressure forces out the cocoa butter, which is then removed by filters. The remaining pressed cake is cooled, further pulverized, and then sifted into cocoa powder.

COCOA BEANS' HIDDEN TREASURES

When cocoa beans are gathered during harvesting, other miscellaneous items or particles often find their way into the mix. These particles sometimes go through fermentation and drying with the beans, and end up packaged in the cocoa bean sacks that are shipped to chocolate manufacturers. When the bags arrive at the factory, the manufacturers often discover interesting items inside. Over the years a multitude of objects have been found, from little metal bowls to small bags of money, and once even a diamond ring.

Vanilla beans, sugar, and roasted cocoa beans

CHOCOLATE LIQUOR'S DESTINY

Eating chocolate is created when chocolate liquor goes through a prerefiner made of a series of heavy rollers set one atop another. The mixture is finely ground down to a specific particle count measured in microns, generally between 15 and 20 microns. The human tongue can detect particle matter at 24 microns. Therefore, a lower micron count yields a smoother chocolate with better mouth-feel.

Conching

This flavor-development process is the next crucial step in making eating chocolate, and can vary in length of time from manufacturer to manufacturer. At this point, cocoa butter is also added. Conching can last from several hours to several days, depending on the desired outcome. During this step, heavy rollers continuously knead the mixture, developing complex flavors and creating a smooth texture; most chocolate manufacturers conch their chocolate between ten and seventy hours. After conching, the mixture is cooled and tempered before being deposited into molds or blocks, or formed into chips or drops. After a quick trip through a cooling tunnel, the solid chocolate is packaged and shipped to a distributor or gourmet store for use and resale.

Not All Chocolate Is Created Equal

Why does all chocolate taste different if the basic process of making chocolate from bean to bar is the same? The answer to this question is complex, because there are so many variables that go into chocolate making. Here are just a few:

- Although cocoa-producing countries have similar climates, there are slight variations from country to country. One region might contain more moisture or humidity than another. This can produce a cocoa tree that is more or less fruitful.

- Variations in climate can also create different methods of agriculture. Each farmer tends to his cacao crop in his own particular way. How the beans are harvested and treated is as important as how they are grown, and both steps can have a direct impact on the final product.

- Roasting and conching times vary greatly depending on manufacturer. A long time and low heat roast with a short conch will generate a different end product than a short time and high heat roast with a long conch.

- The consistency of cocoa butter in each bean depends on how close to the equator the cacao tree is grown. Cocoa butter can fall into several categories, ranging from soft to very hard. The closer to the equator, the harder the cocoa butter. During the chocolate-making process, cocoa butter is added during conching. Harder cocoa butters will produce a harder chocolate, and vice versa. Harder chocolate has a higher melting point than soft chocolate.

- After conching, other ingredients such as milk powder, crumb (milk powder dried at high heat until natural sugars caramelize), or natural caramel flavoring are added. Each company adds their own ingredients to make their chocolate stand apart.

- The type of bean used plays a very large role. As noted earlier, there are three different types of cocoa beans from which all chocolate is made: Criollo, Forastero, and Trinitario. Criollo are the prized beans. They are the most sought after and are believed to produce the best flavor, and therefore the best tasting, chocolate. A less hearty plant than other varieties, this species of cacao tree produces fewer pods overall, with fewer seeds in each. Forastero beans account for most of the world's production. While hearty, these beans produce a chocolate with a less pronounced flavor, meaning they are generally blended with other beans. Trinitario beans account for the smallest percentage of production and are a natural blend of the Criollo and Forastero.

It's no wonder that, with all the variables that go into the chocolate-making process and the vast amount of knowledge needed to understand how each component can affect another, each company's specific chocolate formulas are trade secrets, kept under lock and key!

Single Origins vs. Blends

Single-origin chocolates are those whose beans come from one origin. The meaning of the word *origin*, however, is quite subjective. To one manufacturer, having "one origin" could mean that all the beans are from one area or region, while another manufacturer might define that same term to mean the beans all come from the same, single crop. Sometimes the word *varietal* is used in place of *origin*.

Blends are exactly that—a mix of different beans from different regions and different crops. Blends can contain any number of differences and are not relegated to specific numbers of beans.

Flavor Variations in Artisanal Chocolates

Smaller chocolate companies and artisanal chocolate manufacturers often produce inconsistent chocolate because they cannot usually buy beans in volume. Larger companies can purchase enough beans to continually produce the same chocolate, whereas a smaller manufacturer might only be able to buy a minimum amount of beans from one crop. When they run out and need to buy more, that bean may no longer be available for purchase from that same farmer.

Some companies bypass this challenge by making a bean blend, such as a nine- or twelve-bean blend. This means that they might use some Criollo, some Forastero, and some Trinitario beans when creating their chocolate. But keep in mind that the Criollo beans could come from three different regions in Venezuela, the Forastero from three different farms, and the Trinitario from three different countries. All these beans are then combined in a particular balance to make a specific blend. Yet, because so many beans with so many variables are used, it won't make that much of a difference if at some point one bean in the blend is substituted for another; the overall end result of the chocolate is kept consistent. Only experienced scientists or chocolate makers really know and understand how to create these blends, each with their own subtle flavors.

Percentages

The current trend in labeling chocolate, both for the professional and more recently for the consumer, has been to add a percentage to the name of the chocolate or to the label, such as 72 percent dark chocolate or a 38 percent milk chocolate. This is really just a fancy way of telling the end user how much pure cocoa bean is in that particular chocolate. Here's what you need to remember: the greater the number, the higher the percentage of cocoa bean and the lower the amount of other ingredients such as sugar, lecithin (an emulsifier), and vanilla. For example, a 61 percent dark chocolate tablet would mean that 61 percent of the entire tablet came from the cocoa bean and the remaining 39 percent comprises other ingredients. Milk chocolates range between 32 percent and 45 percent, while dark chocolates range between 52 percent and 100 percent. Unsweetened chocolate is labeled 100 percent and considered pure chocolate, as it only contains matter from the cocoa bean. But, trust me, you don't want to eat that because it is very bitter!

IS WHITE CHOCOLATE REALLY CHOCOLATE?

A popular misconception is that white chocolate is not actually considered chocolate. But, it is actually chocolate because it contains cocoa fat (not less than 20 percent of its weight) among other ingredients.

Many variables go into creating chocolate. Even if you know that 61 percent of a chocolate tablet came from the cocoa bean, that 61 percent could be broken down in different ways, depending on each individual chocolate manufacturer's formula. One company might use a formula whereby, of the 61 percent in question, 55 percent is chocolate liquor and the other 6 percent is cocoa butter. Another company might use a formula where 48 percent is liquor and the remainder cocoa butter. This is just one of the reasons why, if you taste three different brands of 61 percent chocolate side by side, they each have different flavor and texture profiles.

What Makes a Good Chocolate?

The perfect bean, perfect blend, or perfect chocolate does not exist; it all depends on what each consumer likes best as well as its intended use. Is the chocolate just for eating or also for baking? Some chocolates lose their flavor when baked or frozen in ice cream, whereas others prepared in exactly the same way can overpower. Certain chocolates have a more acidic profile, some are smoother, and some taste more of vanilla. Each manufacturer adds certain nuances that are better suited for different uses. One company may make better cocoa powder or milk chocolate than another.

When choosing a chocolate, be aware of what role it will play in the finished product. Remember that in a pure dark chocolate truffle, the dominant flavor will be the chocolate, so choose one with the flavor profiles you want the truffle to have. If you are baking milk chocolate brownies, on the other hand, the chocolate flavor will be diluted by the flour, butter, and other ingredients, so choose a milk chocolate with a strong enough profile to come through.

These days, consumers have a much wider selection when choosing chocolate for eating, baking, or creating confections. Most gourmet or specialty food stores now carry consumer-friendly versions of the same chocolate used by professional pastry chefs. And if you can't find it at a store nearby, there's always the Internet.

As with all ingredients, the rule to follow when choosing chocolate is to buy the best you can within your budget. A good way to start is to try the plain chocolate to see if you like how it tastes. This may sound obvious, but believe me, if you were to taste test five different dark or milk chocolates in a row, I am sure you would find at least one whose profile you did not care for as much as the others. Also, buy 2–3 times as much as your recipe calls for in case you make mistakes during tempering.

When you taste a piece of chocolate, put it on your tongue and press it up against the roof of your mouth. Let the chocolate dissolve slowly; don't chew it. Allow the melted chocolate to coat your entire mouth and tongue, so that it hits all your taste buds at once. If you are tasting more than one type of chocolate, rinse your mouth with room temperature water in between each chocolate to cleanse your palate.

Unused chocolate is best stored by wrapping it well in plastic wrap and putting it away in your pantry or another cool, dry spot. Never put chocolate in the refrigerator as this is a humid environment that can cause condensation to occur on the surface of the chocolate. You will know this has happened if the chocolate turns white, or blooms. This process is known specifically as sugar bloom. Bloom can also be caused by a drastic temperature change, usually when the chocolate gets too hot, melts, and then cools down and becomes hard once again. In this instance,

CHEF'S CHOICE

For my chocolate production, a brand I use often is E. Guittard, manufactured by the Guittard Chocolate Company near San Francisco. Guittard has recently come out with a consumer line, and their chocolate is consistent and lends itself well to most applications. Generally speaking, some of Guittard's milk chocolates have strong dairy notes and some have pronounced caramel undertones, while their dark chocolates range from a strong sweet "dutched" (alkali-processed) cocoa powder flavor to mildly acidic. Their line of chocolate complements my flavor profiles nicely. Other brands I like are Barry Callebaut, Esprit des Alpes, Felchlin, Michel Cluizel, Weiss, and Valrhona.

Left: sugar bloom; center: properly tempered chocolate; right: fat bloom.

blooming means that the fat has separated from the chocolate and risen to the top. In either case, bloom does not harm the chocolate. Rather, it creates an imperfect appearance. It is still perfectly safe to eat the bloomed chocolate or to use it in baking or candy making.

BLOOMING

Bloom is classified two ways: fat bloom and sugar bloom. Fat bloom happens when chocolate is used that has not been tempered properly. Because the fats are not emulsified, the cocoa butter rises to the surface of the chocolate and sets, giving the chocolate a white and milky appearance. Sugar bloom creates the same physical appearance but is caused by condensation on the surface of the chocolate. Condensation happens, for example, when you store chocolate in the refrigerator, a cold and humid environment. Upon removing the chocolate to a warmer room, condensation occurs due to the change in temperature. When the water evaporates, the sugar content in the chocolate crystallizes on the surface, causing a white appearance. Although ugly in appearance, both types of bloomed chocolate are flavorful and safe to eat.

Other Ingredients

You've heard this before, but it's worth repeating: garbage in, garbage out. Use the best ingredients you can buy within your budget. If you're going to take the time to make chocolate, don't skimp on anything. One inferior-quality ingredient can make your homemade chocolate mediocre. What follows here is a list of basic ingredients other than chocolate that are used for making chocolates and confections. Use this list as your starting point, but don't be afraid to experiment with other ingredients to concoct your own creations.

Alcohols

As with any other ingredient, try to buy the best-quality liquors and liqueurs you can find, as this can directly affect the flavor of the final chocolate. If a recipe calls for Grand Marnier, use Grand Marnier, not an orange-flavored Cognac or a knockoff. When using bourbon, use an aged variety that is well known. Basically, only use an alcoholic ingredient that you would enjoy drinking.

Butter

The best choice for butter, in my opinion, is one that contains 83 percent butterfat. It has a smooth mouth-feel and a neutral flavor, and is very consistent from batch to batch. As with heavy cream, the higher the fat percentage, the lower the water content, so use as high a percentage as you can find. These days, most gourmet or specialty stores carry a variety of butters from around the world. Find one whose taste you like and whose butterfat comes as close to 80 percent as possible. And, while it may seem counterintuitive, I prefer to use salted butter in most of my recipes, as the salt positively affects the flavor of the recipe.

Fruit Purée vs. Fresh Fruit

Fruit and chocolate are a great combination. I prefer to use purée instead of fresh fruit as the purée provides flavor and quality consistency throughout the entire year. If you cannot find fresh frozen purée, then buy the best quality and ripest fruit possible. With the exception of berries, any fruit that has a skin needs to be peeled first. Purée the fruit in a food processor or blender until completely smooth and use a scale to ensure an accurate weight on your purée. Weigh out enough confectioners' sugar to equal 10 percent of the total weight of the purée (for every 10 ounces of purée add 1 ounce of sugar). Return the purée and the confectioners' sugar to the food processor or blender, and mix until smooth and well combined. Strain the purée through a fine-mesh sieve before using to remove seeds or impurities.

Heavy Cream

In a ganache recipe, heavy cream is almost as important as the chocolate. If you aren't sure which brand of heavy cream to use, test a variety of brands to see what tastes best to you. I prefer to use a 40 percent heavy cream due to its low water content. The

Always taste your butter before you use it in a recipe. Sometimes a herd of dairy cows will come across a patch of wild onions in a pasture. Believe it or not, this flavor comes out in their milk and in the resulting butter, and no one wants chocolate that tastes like onions!

Fruit purée provides flavor consistency year round.

GANACHE

Ganache is an emulsion between chocolate and heavy cream or milk. Most ganaches are made by heating the liquid until it just begins to boil. The hot liquid is then poured over chopped chocolate. As the chocolate melts from the heat of the liquid, the mixture is slowly and carefully combined to form an emulsion. As with butter, the fat content of the cream has a direct correlation to the finished chocolate: the higher the fat content, the richer the ganache.

higher number means more fat and less water. I also try to use heavy cream that is ultrapasteurized, meaning it is exposed to higher heat in processing, which further limits bacteria growth.

Herbs

Certain herbs can bring out nuances in chocolate. I don't use earthy herbs such as sage, parsley, and chives because they are too strong in flavor and would overwhelm the chocolate. Floral herbs such as lavender, basil, lemon verbena, rosemary, and mint, however, are good choices because they are not dominant: they combine well with other flavors and have multiple applications. I only use fresh, culinary-grade herbs, never dried. Fresh herbs contain natural oils and water, which account for much of their flavor. This natural flavor is removed along with the moisture content when the herbs are dried. When you buy dried herbs, you also have no idea how long ago they were dried and therefore how strong their flavor is. Using fresh herbs guarantees a much more consistent end result.

Nuts

Tree fruits, commonly referred to as nuts, are one of the earth's greatest gifts. Different nuts work well with different chocolates depending on their flavor profiles and fat content. For example, oily nuts work well when making pralines, as oil is needed to create a smooth consistency.

Nuts are a very versatile ingredient. They can be puréed into cream, adding flavor to a ganache; made into a nut paste for added texture; or crushed and used for decoration on the outside of a chocolate. Always use unsalted nuts and be sure to remove any shells. If possible, buy nuts that are hot-air toasted. If you can't find those, buy raw nuts and toast them in the oven until their center is a deep, dark golden brown. This brings out the full, natural flavor of the nut. Toasted nuts always have more flavor than raw nuts. Try not to buy fried nuts, as frying changes the flavor, adds unwanted oils, and can cause the nuts to go rancid more quickly. Leftover nuts should be stored in an airtight container in the refrigerator.

Fresh rosemary, mint, basil, and thyme

Using all-natural oils, such as habanero oil made from fresh habanero peppers, is a great way to create new flavor profiles.

Oils and Natural Flavorings

When flavoring a ganache or any type of chocolate confection, use only all-natural flavorings or oils, never artificial products. A wide selection of culinary-grade all-natural flavors and oils are readily available through gourmet or specialty stores or via the Internet. Almost any flavor you want can be found in an oil-base form, and most are priced within reason. All-natural flavorings tend to be more expensive than artificial but are worth every penny. Try the same flavor in a few different brands to see which one you prefer. With oils and natural flavorings, you might find that you prefer using a variety of brands to get a variety of results.

Salt

To salt or not to salt? Salt naturally brings out the flavor of the medium that is being used and this holds true for chocolate. One of my favorite combinations is a bitter caramel made with Sel de Guerande. This is a sea salt hailing from Brittany, on the northwest coast of France. I prefer sea salt instead of iodized salt as it contains less sodium, meaning it has a less medicinal flavor. Look for sea salt that is packed with a small amount of moisture to ensure its freshness, and once opened keep it in an airtight container.

Sel de Guerande, a coarse sea salt from Brittany, France

FLAVORED SALTS

I have recently noticed gourmet stores and catalogs carrying a variety of flavored salts. Many of these are also different colors, ranging from light green to a deep, dark red.

Spices, from left to right: coriander seeds, chile powder, fennel seeds, curry powder, and cardamom seeds.

Spices

If you are not familiar with any particular brand of spices, buy the same spice manufactured by a few different brands and taste them side by side. Not all spices are the same. I've made chocolate using cayenne pepper from one source and cayenne pepper from another, and one chocolate was twice as hot as the other. This rule applies to all spices.

A good spice to taste test is cinnamon. If it creates a slight amount of heat on your tongue and tastes peppery, that means it is fresh. You can then assume that the spice company purchases good-quality cinnamon sticks and turns its product over quickly. Chances are, other spices made by the same company will be equally good.

Vanilla

Whenever possible, use fresh vanilla beans. There are two types of vanilla beans on the market: Bourbon and Tahitian. If you can find both types, try each one to determine which you like best. I prefer using a combination of two parts Bourbon to one part Tahitian. If you must use vanilla extract, make sure it is all-natural, not imitation. Keep in mind that by using an extract you are adding water to the recipe, which increases your chances of bacterial growth.

To remove the seeds from a vanilla bean, first slice the bean in half lengthwise. Then simply run the blade of a paring knife from one end of the split bean to the other, while applying firm pressure to the blade. The seeds will mound up on the blade of the knife.

Water

When it comes to making chocolate, water is the enemy and the main cause of bacterial growth. The lower the water activity level, the less likely bacteria will grow. Bacterial growth equals mold. This is especially true for chocolates and confections made without the addition of preservatives. This does not mean that all moisture must be removed from these chocolates. It simply means that moisture content must be controlled.

It is difficult to predict the shelf life of any preservative-free product. Proper storage plays a large role in extending that life. Unless stated otherwise, the chocolates and confections in this book should be stored in an airtight container at 60°F to 65°F (15.5°C to 18.3°C) for no longer than two weeks.

TIP:

Here's a trick used by pastry chefs worldwide: Because vanilla beans are so expensive, don't throw the bean away once you've removed the seeds. Instead, stick it in a jar with sugar and let it dry. The sugar will absorb the flavor of the vanilla and you will be left with vanilla sugar. When the vanilla bean has dried completely, you can also grind it together with the sugar in a food processor, for a stronger-flavored vanilla sugar. Use this in place of regular sugar in any recipe where you want to add a subtle vanilla flavor.

Chapter Two

TECHNIQUES

What does it mean to temper and why is it necessary? When you buy a candy bar at the store and break it apart, you may notice that it has a slight snap or crunch. That candy bar is tempered. If you buy a bag of chocolate chips to use in cookies, those chips are tempered. The chocolate coating on the outside of any commercial candy bar is tempered. But what exactly does that signify? Tempering is the process of melting chocolate, cooling it down, and heating it up again slightly. Basically, it is raising and lowering the temperature of melted chocolate so that the fat crystals in the cocoa butter stabilize. That's a simplified scientific explanation. The practical one is that you are simply adjusting the characteristics of the melted chocolate so that it sets up with a nice glossy shine, doesn't melt in your hands upon contact, has a pleasing texture when eaten, and melts nicely on the tongue.

This chapter presents techniques for learning to melt and temper chocolate. There is a lot of information out there about how to do this; other books on chocolate may contain slightly different information. This is simply how I do it and the way that works best for me. If you have experience with tempering and are comfortable with a different method, use the one you prefer.

Tempering

If you have never tempered chocolate before, don't get discouraged if it doesn't work right away. Likewise, if you get it right the first go around, don't assume that will be the case every time. A lot of factors go into the tempering process beyond just the actual type or brand of chocolate

TEMPERED VS. UNTEMPERED

Tempered chocolate sets quickly at room temperature, hardens as it dries, is shiny and brittle, shrinks slightly as it sets (and therefore releases easily from a mold), has a smooth mouth-feel, and, once set, holds its luster and shape at room temperature for extended amounts of time without melting. However, once reheated past a certain temperature, the chocolate will melt, and at that point it is no longer tempered. Untempered chocolate dries very slowly at room temperature, is tacky to the touch, sticks to the inside of a mold, has a cakey texture when eaten, and usually has a blotchy appearance.

used. For example, it is generally easier to temper chocolate in a cool, dry environment than in a warm, humid one. This pertains to not just the climate inside the room where you are tempering but also to the weather outside. Keep in mind that different brands and types of chocolate temper differently. What works with one may not work for all. The temperature range needed to melt and temper one type and brand of chocolate may not be the same as for another. The best advice I can give you is to keep trying. Eventually, experience will win and you will recognize when the chocolate is working with you or against you, and you will be able to adjust your techniques as needed. Also, temper the chocolate as close as possible to the time you'll be using it, as it doesn't hold indefinitely.

How to Melt and Temper Chocolate

Now that you have a basic idea of the tempering process, let's get started. Depending on what brand of chocolate you are using, you may need to chop it first. A heavy, serrated chef's knife with a 10" (25 cm) blade generally works best for this. Place the block of chocolate on a clean cutting board. Start at one corner of the block and slice it on the diagonal instead of straight on. Try to keep the chopped pieces similar in size, not to exceed ½" (1.3 cm) chunks.

Tempering takes place in stages, so here I will try to break it down into steps to make it less confusing.

Step One: Prepping the Chocolate

Place approximately 75 percent of the chopped chocolate called for in the recipe into a glass bowl. Keep in mind you will be adding more chocolate to the bowl after the initial amount is melted; use a large enough bowl so that you are able to stir easily without spilling its contents. The remaining 25 percent of chocolate should be chopped further into smaller pieces and set aside to be used during the "seeding" process, the step that takes place after melting.

Step Two: Melting the Chocolate

Once you have 75 percent of the chopped chocolate in the glass bowl, you have two options for melting: microwave or double boiler.

Microwave Method

This is my preferred method of melting chocolate, because it is practical and time efficient. Place the glass bowl in the microwave and heat at 60-second intervals with the power set on medium (50 percent). Keep in mind that microwaves vary in power from brand to brand, so pick a power level that is roughly half of full power. The amount of time you will need to melt the chocolate will depend on the strength of your microwave and the amount of chocolate in the bowl. Open the microwave door and stir the chocolate with a rubber spatula between each 60-second heating.

Heat the chocolate to between 115°F and 120°F (46°C and 49°C). As soon as the chocolate has reached the proper temperature range, remove it from the microwave. Be careful not to overheat it; you do not want to burn the chocolate. At this point the melted chocolate should be fairly smooth with few, if any, lumps. Stir the melted chocolate very well and set the bowl aside for about 10 minutes. If you do overheat the chocolate and it burns, you will need to throw that batch away and start over. You will be able to tell the chocolate has burned by its scorched smell!

Double-Boiler Method

This method seems to be preferred by most home bakers as it offers a bit more control over temperature fluctuations. I rarely use a double boiler when tempering chocolate, as I do not like to have hot water around when working with chocolate—it increases the chances of accidentally mixing water or steam into the melting chocolate. As I have said before, water is the enemy of chocolate. The addition of water in the form of steam at this stage of the

TIP:

I use a laser thermometer that I bought at one of the major home improvement chains, so I can get a digital readout. You can also use a candy thermometer to check the temperature of the melted chocolate; just remember to hold the thermometer in the center of the bowl and do not let it rest on the bottom.

In my kitchen, I let the warm chocolate sit for about 2 hours, but that is not practical in a home kitchen. Allowing the chocolate to sit for 10 minutes helps ensure that all the fat and sugar crystals have completely separated. This will help you get a good temper. Also, the residual heat in the melted chocolate will fully melt any remaining lumps.

tempering process will cause the chocolate to seize. You will know this has happened if the melted chocolate goes from smooth to grainy and stiff within seconds. If this happens, you will need to start over with a clean, dry bowl and fresh chocolate. The size of the glass bowl holding the chopped chocolate will dictate what size saucepot to use as the bottom part of the double boiler. Use a saucepot whose lip comes about halfway up the side of the glass bowl and allows the glass bowl to sit suspended, without its bottom touching the water in the pot.

Fill the saucepot with enough water to create heat and steam, yet not enough to touch the bottom of the glass bowl. Bring the water to a rolling boil, uncovered. Remove the saucepot from the stovetop and set it on the counter or another heatproof surface. Place the glass bowl of chopped chocolate on top of the steaming water and let sit. The indirect heat of the steam will melt the chocolate. Stir the chocolate occasionally as it melts. If the water cools down too much, set the glass bowl aside and reheat the water before proceeding. Melt the chocolate until it registers a temperature between 115°F and 120°F (46°C and 49°C) as specified in the microwave method section and set the bowl aside for 10 minutes.

Step Three: Seeding the Chocolate

After the 10 minutes have passed, give the chocolate a good stir. You will now move into the actual tempering process. Take the remaining 25 percent of finely chopped chocolate that was set aside earlier and add it by the handful to the warm, melted chocolate. This is called seeding the chocolate because you are adding seeds (finely chopped chocolate) to the melted chocolate. Slowly

SEEDING CHOCOLATE

The cold chocolate performs two functions during this stage: it helps lower the temperature of the warm, melted chocolate (just like when you add ice to a liquid and the liquid cools down) and it helps to realign the molecular structure of the melted chocolate by creating an emulsion.

Seeding the chocolate

incorporate each handful of chopped chocolate into the melted chocolate by stirring it in completely until smooth.

You may or may not need all of the remaining cold chocolate to bring the larger amount of melted chocolate into temper. Using a thermometer, test the liquid chocolate after fully incorporating each handful of chopped chocolate. If you are tempering dark chocolate, the temperature you are trying to achieve is 86°F (30°C). Milk and white chocolates need to reach 81°F (27°C).

Once the proper temperature is reached, stop seeding, even if you have some of the remaining chocolate left over. Likewise, if you have used up all the finely chopped chocolate and the melted chocolate has not cooled down sufficiently, you will need to finely chop more chocolate and continue to slowly add it in. If the liquid chocolate has reached the desired temperature and still contains lumps, use an immersion blender to smooth it out. Place the blade of the immersion blender into the center of the bowl of chocolate and carefully move it in circles as it blends. Make sure you don't tip the side of the blade up and out of the liquid, or it will splatter chocolate all over you and your kitchen!

TIP:

During this part of the process, if I am using a candy thermometer, I generally leave it in the bowl as I stir the chocolate. That way I can keep an eye on how the temperature of the chocolate fluctuates. When using a digital thermometer, simply take the temperature reading after incorporating each handful of chopped chocolate.

An immersion blender will help to remove lumps.

It sounds confusing to melt, heat, cool down, and now reheat the chocolate. Trust me, you need to follow this step in order to complete the process that takes place on a molecular level in order to end up with tempered chocolate.

Step Four: Reheating the Chocolate

Once the liquid chocolate has cooled down to the desired temperature, it needs to be reheated slightly to finish the tempering process.

This is the tricky part. You will need to heat the bowl of chocolate in the microwave for anywhere from 1 to 5 seconds, depending on the power of your unit. If you are using a double boiler, follow the same procedure as earlier to heat the water in the double boiler, and place the bowl of cooled chocolate over the water in 10- to 20-second increments, stirring between each heating. Proceed slowly and keep in mind that the melted chocolate holds residual heat inside and that this residual heat will continue to raise the overall temperature of the chocolate. When tempering dark chocolate, bring the temperature back up to 89°F (32°C). The ideal temperature for milk and white chocolates is 86°F (30°C).

Testing for Temper

Now that you have gone through all the hassle, you want to make sure your chocolate is tempered before you use it. One quick way to test for temper is to drizzle a small amount of the chocolate onto a piece of parchment or waxed paper. You can also dip the tip of a paring knife into the chocolate and set it aside on the counter. If tempered, the chocolate on the paper or knife will set in less than 5 minutes, and it will be shiny and glossy.

Be aware of a false temper. This can happen if the temperature sequence was off during the tempering process, if the room is too cold or hot, if the chocolate has sat too long and gone out of temper, or a combination of any of the above. A practiced eye can soon tell if this has happened. Pour a wide strip of chocolate onto parchment or waxed paper. Next, draw your finger through the chocolate in one swipe. If the line is clean and holds its shape, it is tempered. If the sides appear grainy and uneven, look closer.

When tempered properly, chocolate sets up quickly.

Chances are, you will see that while the top layer of chocolate has set, the cocoa butter underneath has separated.

Hold Your Temper

Now that you have actually tempered the chocolate, you will need to know how to hold it in temper long enough to complete your recipe. Unfortunately, there is not a formula to predict how long it will take for a bowl of chocolate to fall out of temper. Once again, many variables come into play: the brand of chocolate, the size of the bowl and the amount tempered, and the temperature in the room, to name a few. The larger the volume of chocolate tempered, the longer the temper will hold. For this reason, it is generally easier to temper more chocolate than you will actually need to complete the recipe. The unused chocolate can be cooled when finished and stored for future use. Try to temper the chocolate as close as possible to the time you will need to use it. Once the chocolate is tempered, keep a close eye on the side of the bowl as that is the first place you will begin to see the chocolate set. If you do see this begin to happen, use a hair-dryer set on medium heat to "flash" the chocolate for 5 to 8 seconds at a time, while stirring continuously. This small amount of heat will bring the chocolate back to the proper temperature if it has cooled down only slightly.

Once the chocolate is tempered, make sure you do not over-heat it when attempting to rewarm it. If the chocolate heats to over 90°F (32°C), the temper will break and cause separation of the crystallized fats and sugars. And then you will have to start all over again!

Left: proper temper;
Right: false temper

Once tempered, chocolate will first begin to harden and lose its temper on the side of the bowl.

Ideal Temperatures for Tempering

The manufacturers of the following brands of chocolate recommend using the corresponding temperatures when working with their chocolate. You can use this information as a guide to help you temper your chocolate properly.

Brand	Melting Temperature	Seeding Temperature	Working Temperature
Barry Callebaut/Cacao Barry Dark	113-122°F (40-45°C)	81°F (27°C)	87.8°F (31°C)
Barry Callebaut/Cacao Barry Milk	104-113°F (45-50°C)	81°F (27°C)	84-86°F (29-30°C)
Barry Callebaut/Cacao Barry White	104-113°F (40-45°C)	81°F (27°C)	82-84°F (27-29°C)
E. Guittard 61%	115°F (46°C)	88°F (31°C)	89-91°F (31-33°C)
E. Guittard 38%	110°F (43°C)	85°F (29°C)	86-88°F (30-31°C)
E. Guittard 31%	110°F (43°C)	85°F (29°C)	86-88°F (30-31°C)
Esprit Des Alpes Amber 38% Double Cream	110°F (43°C)	79°F (26°C)	84-86°F (29-30°C)
Esprit Des Alpes Garnet 63% Dark	115°F (46°C)	81°F (27°C)	86-88°F (30-31°C)
Esprit Des Alpes Opal White	110°F (43°C)	79°F (26°C)	84-86°F (29-30°C)
Felchlin Dark	113-122°F (45-50°C)	83-86°F (28-30°C)	90°F (32°C)
Felchlin Milk	113-122°F (45-50°C)	83-86°F (28-30°C)	88°F (31°C)
Felchlin White	113-122°F (45-50°C)	83-86°F (28-30°C)	86°F (30°C)
Michel Cluizel Grand Lait 45%	106°F (40°C)	78°F (26°C)	86-88°F (30-31°C)
Michel Cluizel Ivoire 37%	106°F (40°C)	76°F (25°C)	84-86°F (29-30°C)
Michel Cluizel Plantation Los Anconés 67%	116°F (45°C)	80°F (27°C)	88-90°F (31-32°C)
Michel Cluizel Noir 85%	116°F (45°C)	80°F (27°C)	88-90°F (31-32°C)
Weiss Lait Entier 37%	113-115°F (45-46°C)	79-81°F (26-27°C)	82-86°F (27-30°C)
Weiss Nevea 29%	111-113°F (44-45°C)	77-79°F (25-26°C)	81-84°F (27-29°C)
Weiss Tribago 64%	131-133°F (55-56°C)	84-88°F (29-31°C)	90-91°F (32-33°C)

Recipe Notes

Once you have mastered the basic recipes, use the information to create your own unique creations. The fun confections detailed in chapter eight are product specific and should be followed as such.

Measurements

All the recipes in this book contain three different measurements: ounces, cups, and grams. Professional recipes are always written in weight (ounces or grams) as weight measurement is more accurate than volume (cups and table/teaspoons). I recommend weighing all ingredients using a digital scale and frequently checking the calibration. You can use a scale that measures in either ounces or grams, and weights have been included for both. I highly recommend that you use the gram measurements if at all possible, as those will give you the most precise results. Even though all the recipes were tested thoroughly, there can often be slight differences when converting weight measurements. If you cannot find or do not have a scale that measures in grams, then use the ounce measurement next. Only use the cup and spoon measurements if you are unable to use a scale.

Recipes in this book calling for chocolate, cocoa butter, and nuts will list required amounts by weight only, in both ounces and grams. Quantities by cup measurement have been omitted for the sake of accuracy. How large or small your chocolate or cocoa butter is chopped, or the size of nuts used, will dictate how much will fit into a cup measure. Because everyone chops differently, cup measurements vary too much by individual to guarantee the recipes' results.

Chocolate Substitutions

All the recipes in this book, regardless of whether they call for white, milk, or dark chocolate, list the chocolate by cocoa bean percentage. As mentioned in chapter one, the higher the percentage, the darker the chocolate. If you would like to adjust a recipe for a slightly darker or lighter chocolate, don't vary the percentage by more than 5 percent in either direction. For example, don't substitute a 55 percent chocolate when the recipe calls for a 72 percent, and vice versa.

Yields

The recipes in this book have been adapted and tested for the home kitchen. Although they are scaled down significantly from a commercial kitchen, they do have generous product yields, and you will surely find lots of friends and family to help you eat all the yummy treats you make!

Because these recipes are so precise, do not try to double them or scale them back to make a smaller batch. If you want to make more chocolates or confections than the recipe yields, you will need to make the recipe over again as many times as necessary to create the amount of finished product you desire.

Working with Hot Sugar

You will be working with hot sugar to make the caramels in this book. Be extremely careful as hot sugar sticks to the skin and can cause severe burns. To make the caramel filling, proceed slowly and be careful of possible splattering.

Recipes that use hot sugar may call for small Silpats (11½" x 16½" [29.2 x 41.9 cm]). Silpats are silicone mats used often in baking and candy making and can be easily found in baking supply stores.

Lemongrass-Coconut, page 93 and Ginger Crunch, page 140

How to Make Ganache

Because the technique for making a good ganache is the same no matter what type you are creating, the basic information is included here rather than in each chapter. Once you've mastered this technique, you're well on the way to making many of the recipes in this book.

Tip:

To fix a broken ganache, do the following: place approximately 1 tablespoon (15 ml) of the broken ganache in a small, clean, dry bowl. Bring approximately 2 tablespoons (30 ml) of corn syrup to a boil. While constantly whisking the small amount of ganache, slowly drizzle in about half of the hot corn syrup. (You will only use half of the corn syrup. However, you need to boil double the amount to keep it from crystallizing before you add it to the ganache.) Once the new mixture is emulsified, slowly incorporate the old, broken ganache into the new, emulsified one.

Ganache

The most important factor to keep in mind when making any type of ganache is that you are making an emulsion of ingredients. Think mayonnaise—that's what you want a ganache to look like—creamy, shiny, and thick. While many ganache recipes call for only heavy cream and chocolate, I almost always add butter to my ganache. Butter adds fat to a ganache and acts as a textural agent. Adding butter to ganache makes it creamier and gives the ganache a better mouth-feel. Keep in mind that incorporating butter into or removing it from a ganache recipe is not a matter of simply using it or not as desired. The fat content of the chocolate and the heavy cream need to be taken into account and the recipe properly balanced for the ganache to emulsify. White chocolate ganache, for example, generally does not call for butter as the chocolate contains enough fat on its own.

When you make ganache, always start with chopped, not melted, chocolate. To this you will add hot heavy cream, milk, or other liquids depending on the recipe. The heat of the liquid will cause the chocolate to melt. As the chocolate melts into the hot liquid, those two ingredients need to be slowly and carefully combined to create one homogenous mixture. Once the mixture is smooth, the butter is added and gently but fully incorporated.

While it sounds simple, making ganache involves its own small challenges. For instance, if you heat the liquid too much or add hot liquid to melted instead of chopped chocolate, the ganache will separate. Similarly, if you add melted butter instead of merely softened butter to the incorporated mixture, the ganache will separate. And if you over stir while incorporating any of the ingredients, it will break!

1. Pour the hot liquid into the chopped chocolate to melt it.

2. Combine slowly to form an emulsion.

3. Add the butter once the chocolate and cream are fully combined.

4. Left, broken ganache; right, emulsified ganache.

Chapter Three

FLAVOR FUSIONS

F lavor separates a forgettable piece of chocolate from one whose taste you can still conjure up weeks later. Creating good flavor combinations relies as much on your imagination as it does on your knowledge of what ingredients work well together. While to some extent that knowledge is innate, this chapter will try to give you the basics to creating unique combinations.

Traditional Flavor Combinations

If you aren't sure what traditional flavor combinations are, take a look at a chocolate sampler found in a department store or at the selection featured in one of the larger commercial chocolate chains. For the most part, those flavors represent the only type of chocolate that was widely available until very recently: caramels, both chewy and creamy; vanilla cream centers; mint-, raspberry-, or strawberry-filled centers; and crunchy nuts. In Europe, you can still find liquid liqueur-filled centers molded into dark chocolate.

When creating traditional flavored chocolates, keep it simple. Do not try to incorporate too many flavors into one piece. For example, just as raspberry complements chocolate, so does coffee. However, raspberry, coffee, and chocolate do not work well together, because raspberry and coffee are not complementary.

Right: Fresh raspberries and wasabi powder, page 144

Current Trends

What started the unusual chocolate combination movement? Is it due to the recent crossover of pastry chefs into chocolatiers? Is it because it has become easier to obtain different ingredients from around the world? Have chocolatiers simply become more creative? Or is this trend being driven by the press? And what is the deal with habanero peppers and ancho chiles? Our store is constantly bombarded with requests for chocolates made with these ingredients. When we ask our customers why they want those flavors, most respond that they have read about these types of chocolates and therefore want to try them. Or they reference the film *Chocolat*. Who knew that one movie would start a flavor revolution!

On the positive side, the present use of interesting and unusual ingredients in chocolate has forced the industry as a whole to reinvent itself. From small artisan chocolate makers to large industrial companies, they are all coming out with new chocolates in response. The most popular flavor profiles include chiles to add spice; black or pink peppercorns that impart a smoky, fiery taste; savory herbs and spices such as lemongrass, rosemary, cumin, curry, and basil; unusual tropical fruits; and flavored salts. This current trend has encouraged even traditionalists to become more creative with flavors and expand their repertoires. What's in store next? It's anyone's guess as to what direction the trend will take in the future.

TRADITIONAL TASTES

Even though I make it a point to incorporate interesting flavor profiles into each chocolate collection I create, in my personal tastes I lean toward more traditional flavors, such as raspberry, hazelnuts, and Grand Marnier. Call me conventional and old-fashioned, but to me nothing beats a simple yet well-made chocolate whose flavor is well balanced and finishes nicely on the palate.

Nontraditional and Daring Flavor Combinations

Okay, so you want to try your hand at creating new flavor combinations. How to proceed? As stated earlier, expect a lot of trial and error. When trying to incorporate an unusual spice, herb, or other type of flavor into your chocolate, think about what the two will taste like together. For example: think about curry and all of the things curry can accompany: beef, chicken, fish, rice, pasta, and lamb. Curry is actually a very versatile spice and complements chocolate quite well. Sage, however, is only good with a few things because of its overpowering and pungent flavor. Therefore, be cautious with sage and chocolate. Another piece of advice when adding strange and interesting flavor profiles to chocolate: follow the less-is-more theory. If you make a batch of chocolates and feel like the flavor is not quite strong enough, you can always increase it the next time you make the recipe.

So what, exactly, constitutes a nontraditional or daring flavor combination? Personally, I don't think this is limited specifically to whacky flavors. Over the past four years, I have created a number of pieces I would consider to fall into this range without being weird. I am talking about, for example, the candy cane truffle in chapter five and the peanut butter and jam molded chocolate or the candy apple piece in chapter six. Although these flavors are nontraditional in chocolates, they are all adaptations of traditional foods. Candy canes and candy apples are childhood favorites, while peanut butter and jam is a classic pairing. My point is, with a little creativity and balance, there is no limit to the flavor creations you can make.

Finding a Balance

In chocolate making as in cooking, too much of one ingredient can make or break the finished creation. Flavor combinations with chocolate are endless and fine-tuning these combinations takes time, so don't get discouraged if you try one and it doesn't work. Believe me, I have tried plenty of combinations that seemed as if they should pair well but that produced a not-so-tasty result. One combination in particular still baffles me. I often infuse tea into

Chocolate and Herb Pairings

Use this chart as a guide to incorporating commonly used herbs into your own confections.

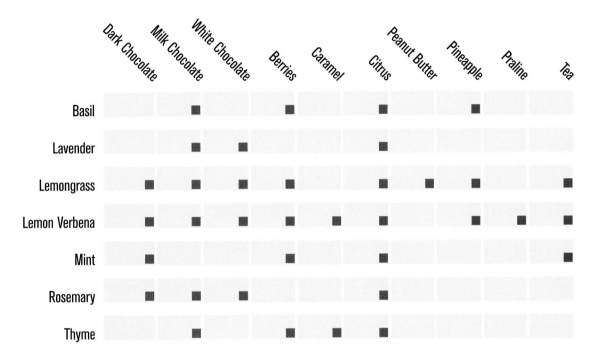

	Dark Chocolate	Milk Chocolate	White Chocolate	Berries	Caramel	Citrus	Peanut Butter	Pineapple	Praline	Tea
Basil		■		■		■		■		
Lavender		■	■			■				
Lemongrass	■	■	■	■		■	■	■		■
Lemon Verbena	■	■	■	■	■	■		■	■	■
Mint	■			■		■				■
Rosemary	■	■	■			■				
Thyme		■		■	■	■				

ganache, as tea in general pairs quite nicely with dark chocolate. With the wide range of tea flavors available on the market, tea combinations are plentiful. I decided to try a Lapsang Souchong tea, which has a dark, assertive, smoky flavor. Unfortunately, the finished chocolate tasted like an ashtray—not quite what I had in mind!

As a general rule, try to combine chocolate with only one or two other flavors as opposed to multiple flavors. A one- or two-flavor combination, when properly balanced, allows for a clean taste in which the flavors and the chocolate are distinct yet complementary. For example, when you bite into a chocolate you taste one flavor, and, as you chew and swallow, you finish with another flavor. It's sort of like tasting in layers. Mixing too many combinations usually results in a muddying of flavors, and the chocolate will taste the same from start to finish.

When I begin the development stage of creating a new piece, I contemplate how well a specific flavor combination might go with chocolate. Oftentimes I find myself eating something, such as toasted sesame seeds, with milk chocolate in my mouth just to see how it will taste. This is a quick and easy way to decide what flavors might work well together without having to go through the exercise of making an entire batch of chocolates.

Sometimes the flavors work and sometimes they don't. Often a flavor or combination might, in fact, taste wonderful with dark, milk, or white chocolate, but won't be practical in an application. Take, for example, a fruit such as cranberry or blueberry. I have yet to make a chocolate with these flavors, incorporating them either as a ganache or a *pâte de fruit* (fruit jelly), due to their water content. As previously mentioned in the ingredients section, water is the number one enemy when making chocolate candies. Water increases bacteria count and limits finished chocolates' shelf life. While I am sure a cranberry or blueberry chocolate would taste great, it would get moldy fairly quickly.

For some time now, hot, spicy, and herbal have been popular flavor profiles. Flavors once relegated to the savory side of the kitchen are more and more often appearing in sweet combinations. This can be wonderful or a complete disaster, depending on how well balanced the final piece is. There are a lot of chocolatiers in the industry who push that envelope when creating nontraditional and daring flavor combinations. These chocolates should be approached with caution. I was once given an anchovy flavored chocolate to try. Need I say more?

Fresh strawberries with balsamic vinegar, page 146

Chocolate and Spice Pairings

Use the following chart as a guide to incorporating commonly used spices into your own confections.

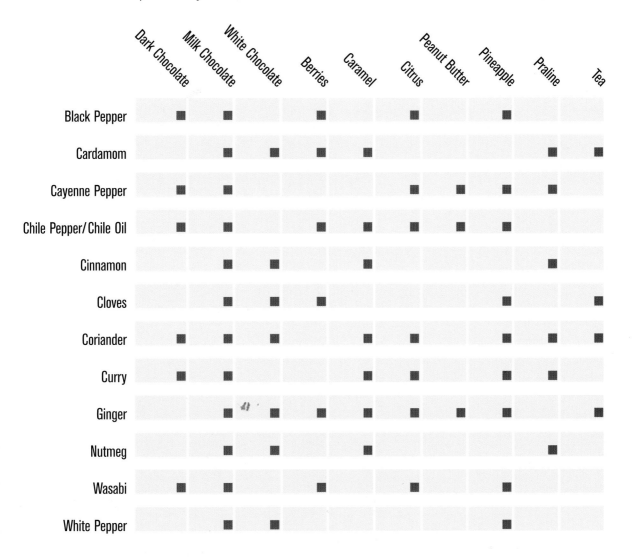

	Dark Chocolate	Milk Chocolate	White Chocolate	Berries	Caramel	Citrus	Peanut Butter	Pineapple	Praline	Tea
Black Pepper	■	■		■		■			■	
Cardamom			■	■	■				■	■
Cayenne Pepper	■		■			■	■		■	■
Chile Pepper/Chile Oil	■	■		■	■	■				
Cinnamon			■	■	■				■	
Cloves			■	■	■				■	■
Coriander	■	■		■	■	■		■	■	■
Curry	■	■			■	■			■	■
Ginger			■	■	■		■			■
Nutmeg			■	■		■			■	
Wasabi	■	■		■			■	■		
White Pepper			■	■					■	

Adding Texture to Flavor

As with any eating experience, chocolate or not, a contrast in texture is equally important as flavor. Texture adds another dimension to the whole experience. Think about it. If you tasted a plain piece of dark chocolate that was completely smooth, and then tasted that same piece of dark chocolate but it had been sprinkled with dark cocoa nibs to add crunch, the flavor experience would be pretty similar but the texture experience would be totally different.

Whenever possible, try to incorporate two different textures into the chocolates you make. Texture can be added to a chocolate in the way of pralines, ground caramel, crisped rice, ground seeds, fruit layers such as jams or cooked jellies or *pâte de fruit* (fruit jellies), and so on. You can even make two different flavors of ganache, one soft and one more dense, to achieve a chocolate with two different textures using the same medium (as in the Triple Espresso-Vanilla piece in chapter six).

When making tablets, such as the fruit and nut ones in chapter eight, I often incorporate raisins, dried fruit, and candied nuts into the bar. That way, when you break off a piece and put it in your mouth, you experience not only the melting chocolate on your tongue but also the soft fruit and crunchy nuts.

So, to quickly recap the general ideas behind flavor and texture:

- Flavor combinations are endless and ideas can be found everywhere.

- Don't try to incorporate too much into one piece.

- Less is more on the flavor-intensity scale.

- Practice makes perfect.

- Not everyone will like everything you make.

- Incorporating texture with flavor adds another dimension.

Have fun; remember—it's just chocolate!

Peanut butter and cayenne pepper, page 102

Chapter Four

PAIRINGS AND PRESENTATION

Everyone has heard of classic food pairings such as wine and cheese, vodka and caviar, or champagne and strawberries. But have you ever heard of wine and chocolate, or beer and chocolate? Not surprisingly, these spirits can work quite well with chocolate when paired properly. Just as a sommelier will match food to wine, so too can chocolate be matched. Interestingly enough, beer also pairs well with chocolate, a fact not many people realize. When the pairing is done well, the flavor and complexity of each balances and complements the other.

With so many wines and beers on the market and so many chocolates now available to the consumer, the best option is to experiment and conduct your own tastings using the guidelines in this chapter.

Trust Your Palate

When you are trying to match chocolate with wine or beer, first take a bite of the chocolate and allow its flavor to fully coat the inside of your mouth. Next, take a sip of the beverage and swirl that around in your mouth. Remember to breathe while you are doing this, as that will enhance the flavors. You can usually tell right away whether something works or not. A bitter or sour taste means the flavors do not mix well together. You are looking more for a buttery, rich sense of flavor more than a distinct flavor profile. If you try a piece of chocolate and follow it with wine or beer and

Right: Port and Sherry with Hazelnut Praline, page 116 and Triple Espresso-Vanilla, page 124

Salted Caramel, page 120, presented in a readily-available salt holder.

White wine with Ginger Crunch, page 140

it leaves a bad taste in your mouth, it probably isn't the right match. Likewise, you will know immediately when it is the right match as all the flavors will blend smoothly in your mouth and taste wonderful together.

If you are serious about pairing your chocolate with wine or beer, keep a log each time you do so. This will allow you to see a pattern on which types of wines generally seem to work best. If your friends sample such combinations, ask them to write down their tasting notes. It's always interesting to see how different people's palates work. Chances are, someone will pick up on a flavor nuance you may have missed.

Pairing Chocolate with Wine

When I was in culinary school, one of the first lessons I learned had to do with salt and pepper. I remember my chef instructor saying that salt and pepper should be sensed in the finished product but they should not be tasted. He was basically saying that, while salt and pepper are needed for balance, one should not be aware that they are present, as their function is simply to enhance and unite the flavors of the dish. The same general idea applies when pairing wine with chocolate. The wine should not overwhelm the chocolate or vice versa, and the flavor nuances in the wine should not fight the flavor nuances in the chocolate. Each should bring out the others' subtle flavors to create a well-rounded experience, where no one flavor dominates over the others.

PAIRING PARTY

As a general rule, the better the ingredients, the better the outcome. This holds somewhat true when pairing wine with chocolate as well. While you don't need to buy the most expensive wine on the market, don't look for the biggest bargain. Where the quality of the wine is important, it is actually the grape or varietal that will

Instead of plastic containers, present Chocolate Shotts™ Cookies, page 152, in unusual and reusable containers.

Remember that paired fla-
vors should complement
rather than imitate each
other. For example, it may
seem like a good idea to
pair a peppery wine with
the peppered pineapple
chocolate in chapter seven.
However, the wine would
most likely enhance the
pepper flavor in the chocolate and overpower the
pineapple, thereby throwing
off the balance of the
piece. And you would be
left with an overall peppery
flavor as a finish.

make the most difference. As with chocolate, different winemakers use different formulas when creating their products. For example, if you find one brand of Merlot that pairs well with a specific piece of chocolate, don't expect every Merlot on the market to pair as nicely with that same piece.

Milk or White Chocolate

The flavor profiles of these types of chocolates generally contain strong dairy notes. Therefore, these chocolates tend to pair well with wines that are a little on the sweet side, such as a Vin de Glacier, a sweet Riesling, a Rancio, or a Sauternes. Imagine crème brûlée—it is topped with sugar that is caramelized. Underneath is the cream. The sugar and the cream go well together; the flavor is very smooth.

White or red wines that are very sour, dry, or acidic will gener-ally not pair well with milk or white chocolate, because acid causes cream to curdle. Imagine eating a salad tossed with a strong vinai-grette and then drinking a glass of milk. Yuck! Nothing in that com-bination is complementary.

Dark Chocolate

Because there are myriad nuances in dark chocolate, many types of wine will work as a pairing. First, determine the flavor profile of the chocolate. Is it bitter, acidic, semisweet, or bittersweet? With any of these, try a bold red wine that is full bodied and fruity. Or, if you prefer, choose a wine that is spicy and peppery. Both would work well because they do not contain a flavor profile that is promi-nent in the chocolate, whereas if you were to pair an acidic wine with an acidic chocolate, the acidity would throw the pairing off balance.

Filled Chocolates

When first attempting to pair chocolate with wine, start with a piece of solid chocolate, or with a chocolate whose center is a pure milk, white, or dark chocolate ganache. You need to first understand and be able to identify what basic flavors work well together before complicating the pairing by adding a filling. This is a lesson that is best learned by trial and error. If you are a wine connoisseur and already have a good sense of balancing wine with food, then you have a head start. If not, just be patient and expect some very interesting experiments.

A creative way to present your chocolates is to lay them on a bed of fragrant spices or other ingredients included in the recipe.

LANGUEDOC-ROUSILLON

The southern region of France, just above the Spanish border, is an area known as Languedoc-Roussillon. Rainfall is low, summers are hot and arid, and winters are very cold. Rugged, steep vineyards dot the countryside and grapes are often harvested late, when their sugar content is quite high. This results in complex, fortified wines that pair extremely well with chocolates.

Fruity Chocolates

These include chocolates made with fruit-flavored ganaches and chocolates that contain *pâte de fruit* (fruit jelly) or jam layers. The addition of the fruit adds acidity to the overall flavor of the chocolate. These go well with Grenache that has been slightly chilled. Red wines with a slightly peppery bite, such as a red Zinfandel, would also work nicely, as would a Pinot Noir low in acid and high in fruit notes. Chardonnay can also work, depending on the amount of oak in the wine and the type of fruit in the chocolate.

Nut Pralines and Centers

Because nut pralines tend to be less sweet than other types of fillings, pair these with a sweeter wine such as a Banyuls, or a fortified wine such as a tawny port or a sherry. Wines that are nutty on the finish, less acidic with a rich, smooth, "buttery" taste at the end, work well.

Pairing Chocolate with Beer

Beer makes for an interesting pairing variation. And while it may sound a bit weird, some chocolate actually pairs really nicely with beer. However, as with wine, the success of the pairing depends completely on the match of the type of beer with the type of chocolate. The possibilities are infinite and it would be impossible to list them all.

As with wine, make an event out of tasting different chocolate and beer pairings. Have an assortment of chocolates on hand, and ask friends to bring favorite brews. Make notes and keep a log, noting what you like and don't like.

When paired correctly, beer and chocolate are pleasing to the palate.

Beer and Chocolate Pairings

Use this chart as a guide when selecting beers to pair with your chocolates. The choices referenced here are personal favorites, but be adventurous, and try other brands of ale, beer, and stout.

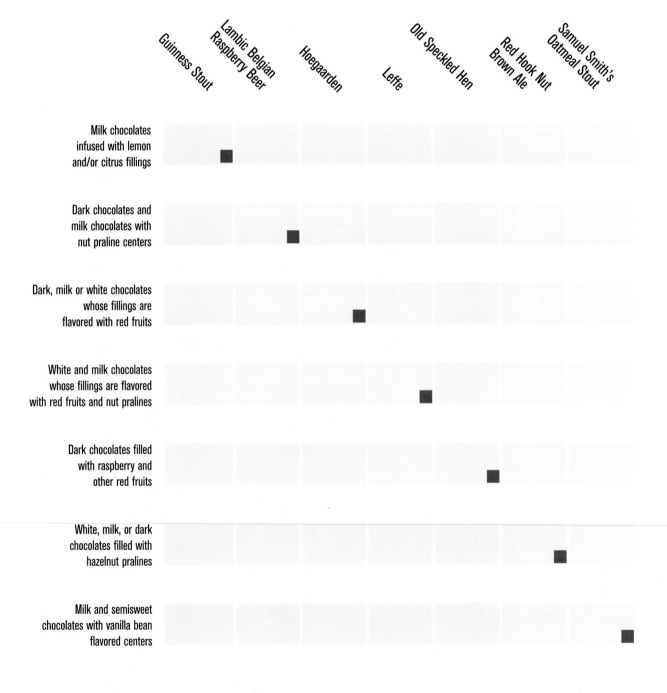

	Guinness Stout	Lambic Belgian Raspberry Beer	Hoegaarden	Leffe	Old Speckled Hen	Red Hook Nut Brown Ale	Samuel Smith's Oatmeal Stout
Milk chocolates infused with lemon and/or citrus fillings		■					
Dark chocolates and milk chocolates with nut praline centers			■				
Dark, milk or white chocolates whose fillings are flavored with red fruits				■			
White and milk chocolates whose fillings are flavored with red fruits and nut pralines					■		
Dark chocolates filled with raspberry and other red fruits						■	
White, milk, or dark chocolates filled with hazelnut pralines							■
Milk and semisweet chocolates with vanilla bean flavored centers							■

Serving Up the Goods

When presenting chocolates and confections to your guests, you can never go wrong with simply laying them out neatly on a serving platter. Not so exciting, but certainly safe and easily understood. Add your own twist to this concept by finding great-looking serving pieces on which to display your chocolates. Keep in mind the overall look and feel of your buffet table or presentation. Consider using any of the following: interestingly shaped mirrors, random pieces of glass tile, remnants of granite or marble, or glass butter dishes as platters. One of my favorite serving pieces is really a leather picture frame whose sides sit about 1" (2.5 cm) above the glass, thereby providing a nice edge. I put interesting pictures inside the frame so, as people eat the chocolate, a scene beneath is revealed.

TIP:

Home improvement stores are great sources for interesting platters. Squares of glass, marble, or tile can be bought inexpensively and made into serving pieces by adding felt feet to their bottom.

Crispy Crunchies, page 160, are presented elegantly on an antique calling-card tray.

Another way to create an interesting look on a simple serving platter is to fill the platter with ingredients used in making the chocolates or confections. For instance, a pile of sugar, a group of vanilla beans, a sculpted lemon, some fresh herbs, and chopped chocolate all together on a platter makes for a gorgeous presentation. Place the chocolates and confections on top of and around all the ingredients, matching those used in their recipes. Not only does this look great, it also smells fantastic.

Keep in mind the colors of the confections you are serving. Many chefs prefer to use stark white plates on which to arrange their food because white highlights, rather than clashes with, the colors of the food. Choose plates that will complement, rather than compete with, the colors and patterns of the chocolates and confections. On the other hand, all-brown chocolates might work well on a colorfully patterned platter. Go ahead, let your inner decorating diva loose!

Presentation

Everyone loves to receive a gift, and those well wrapped or presented in interesting containers tend to be the ones most remembered. When thinking about different ways to present chocolates as gifts, try to create a link between the chocolates and the way they are presented. For example, for a friend's housewarming, I might take a box filled with chocolates, tie it onto a cool pillow, and attach a handmade tag that reads "Sleep well in your new home." Browse through your local department stores and home accessories stores. Keep your eyes open for unique presentation vehicles. Vases, bowls, glasses, candle holders, and boxes can all be used to present chocolate as a gift, and the recipient can reuse the receptacle when the chocolate is gone. Flower pots can be filled with assorted confections and a flower-growing kit that contains a chocolate-colored viola flower for the perfect Mother's Day gift. Similarly, for the fall/winter holidays consider baskets in the shape of a turkey, snowman, or snowflake. Filled with all sorts of goodies, they make a great gift to take to a holiday dinner or party. After, the basket is the perfect size to hold a winter plant or use as a table centerpiece.

Of course, there is nothing more elegant than a simply packaged box or bag with a nice ribbon and bow. Most baking supply stores carry clear, glassine bags best suited for holding all sorts of goodies. A creatively designed handmade tag always adds a touch of fun and whimsy. Because these bags come in a variety of sizes, it is easy to find the one best suited for your use. You may also find interesting containers at local stationary and storage-solution shops.

There really is no limit to how you can present your chocolates. Rifle through your pantry, your basement, or wherever you store items bought on a whim and never used. Let your imagination run wild and be daring. Remember that incorporating different textures and shapes can be visually more interesting.

TIP:

I frequently go to home goods stores just to see what I can find that is new and unusual. The great thing about those stores is that you can often find one or two interesting leftover pieces by themselves instead of having to buy sets. My wife, Tina, often jokes that we have a prop room in our basement.

Part Two

THE CHOCOLATES

I first began making chocolates as a pastry chef working in restaurants in New York City. The chocolates would be sent out to the restaurant patrons at the end of their meal as a thank-you. My first few collections were traditional flavors, simple textures, and not overly imaginative. As I became more experienced, I realized I could have more fun with flavors and I became more adventurous and willing to experiment. Drawing on my classical training, I applied the same philosophy to my chocolates as I did to my desserts: simple, fresh flavors that matched the seasons. If I came across a new product or interesting ingredient, I would often try it out in the chocolates. And as my flavor repertoire grew, so did my use of techniques.

This section of the book will walk you through the three different techniques used to make chocolates: truffles, molded pieces, and hand-dipped. I have also added a chapter called Fun Chocolate Confections. These are some of my personal favorites that can be readily made at home and are great for any age or group or occasion.

Chapter Five

TRUFFLES

Truffles use the most basic techniques and are therefore a good place to start and gain experience. Truffles are also the easiest of the chocolate candies with which to experiment using new flavors by simply altering the flavor of the ganache. Once you have mastered the art of making a ganache it is easy to move on to molded and hand-dipped pieces. However, to be truly successful at producing these three types of chocolates, a thorough understanding of tempering is required, so be sure you are comfortable with that process before proceeding.

Truffles are what most people envision when they think of chocolate candies. They are generally roundish in shape and traditionally found coated in cocoa powder or confectioners' sugar. Modern truffles are often completely smooth and perfectly round, having been dipped in tempered chocolate.

Truffles are fairly simple to make, consisting of a flavored ganache dipped into tempered chocolate and then finished in a variety of dry toppings. Making these can be a great family project, as kids love to roll the ganache into balls before helping to coat and finish them.

What You Will Need to Get Started

You don't really need any special equipment to make your own truffles. The fillings are made in mixing bowls and can either be scooped into balls with a spoon or piped using a pastry bag or sandwich bag with a corner cut out. Dipping the truffles is easier when using a dipping fork but, lacking that, a regular large eating fork will work almost as well. Chances are, most of the equipment you need is probably already in your kitchen waiting to be used. Specialty items such as a dipping fork or pastry bag can be found at local candy-making supply stores or through some of the sources listed at the back of this book.

Classic Dark 72 Percent, page 86

Fillings and Flavors

Generally speaking, truffle centers are smooth, moist, and single-flavored. Truffle varieties are usually achieved by infusing the cream with the desired flavor while making the ganache or by incorporating an oil or alcohol into the ganache while preparing the recipe. Some truffle centers contain nut pieces, which make for an interesting contrast. There is really no limit to what you can use for a filling flavor. A good rule of thumb is, if you can infuse it into the cream or mix it into the finished ganache, it can be used to flavor the truffle. Now, whether or not the taste is pleasing to the consumer, that's a different story!

Truffles can be made in white, milk, or dark chocolate, or a combination thereof, as long as the recipe is well balanced and takes into account the type of chocolate being used. Likewise, the truffles can be finished in almost any type of topping as long as it is complementary to the overall flavor.

The ganache used to make truffles is slightly different than fillings used for other applications. If you are looking at a chart that lists the amount of chocolate and cream used to make a truffle ganache versus ganache used in either a molded chocolate or a hand-dipped chocolate, the truffle ganache would contain approximately 30 percent less heavy cream than molded chocolate ganache and approximately 20 percent less than hand-dipped ganache. This results in a ganache that is slightly more dense and dry, thus allowing it to be piped or rolled into a round shape.

Chocolate truffles get their name from the fungi variety found buried in the ground. This is due to their round, often uneven shape and their dark and dusty appearance.

Truffles

Once the ganache is made and ready to use, it's time to form the truffles. This can be done either by scooping ganache with a spoon or melon baller or by piping the ganache onto a baking sheet or piece of parchment paper and then rolling it into balls by hand. It is faster to pipe than to scoop and roll. If you don't have a pastry bag handy, make your own by using a large sandwich bag. Place the ganache into the bag and push it all down into one of the corners. Then cut an opening out of the corner of the bag. Applying pressure from the top of the bag down, deposit small blobs of truffle ganache onto a baking sheet. Let them sit overnight at room temperature to allow the ganache to dry. This will make the truffles easier to shape. Roll the blobs into balls and they are ready to be dipped and finished.

1. Use a pastry bag to pipe ganache into small blobs.

2. Roll the piped or scooped ganache between your palms to form a smooth ball.

TIP:

If you have access to a candy-making supply store, buy an Ateco 806 plain tip to use when piping the ganache.

Finishing the Truffles

Before you can roll the truffles in the desired topping, they need to be dipped in tempered chocolate. This will make the topping stick to the truffle and give it a thin chocolate outer shell. Truffles can be dipped into white, milk, or dark chocolate, as the recipes dictates. Keep in mind that the chocolate being used to dip the truffles must be tempered to set properly.

As a general rule, almost anything can be used as a topping: finely chopped or ground nuts, cocoa powder, confectioners' sugar, cinnamon sugar, and so on. Keep in mind your topping should somehow reflect or complement the flavor of the truffle. When preparing the topping, be sure to finely chop or shred it into small enough pieces so that it will easily adhere to the outside of the truffle. If the topping size is too big, it will not evenly coat the outside of the truffle, affecting not just the overall flavor of the piece but also its appearance.

The dipping and finishing process is almost one continuous step, so don't try to dip all the truffles at once and then try to roll them in whatever topping is being used. Dip and finish one truffle at a time.

When you dip the truffles, make sure they are fully coated in the tempered chocolate before finishing them by rolling them in the topping. It is generally easier to place the topping in a long, deep pan so that you can easily roll the truffle around in the pan. This will allow the topping to fully coat the truffle.

1. Dip the truffles in tempered chocolate to coat.

2. Roll them in desired topping.

Classic Dark 72 Percent

Pure dark chocolate centers are a classic truffle flavor. The use of a high-percentage dark chocolate modernizes this recipe. A greater percentage of cocoa bean makes the chocolate flavor darker and more pronounced. Rolling the truffles in cocoa powder further emphasizes the deep richness of the chocolate.

This is not a truffle for the faint of heart. If you prefer a less strong chocolate flavor, you can substitute the 72 percent chocolate with a 61 percent. You can also finish the truffles by rolling them in a mixture of cocoa powder and confectioners' sugar to cut back on the intensity of the chocolate.

EASY   **Yield: 30 truffles**

4¼ ounces (119 g) 72 percent extra-bittersweet chocolate, chopped
4 ounces or ½ cup (112 g) heavy cream
½ ounce or 2 teaspoons (14 g) light corn syrup
½ ounce or 1 tablespoon (14 g) salted butter, cubed, soft but not melted

To finish truffles:
9½ ounces or full 2¼ cups (266 g) cocoa powder
1 pound (453 g) 61 percent bittersweet chocolate, tempered

1. To make the ganache: Place the chopped chocolate in a medium-size bowl. Set aside. Combine the heavy cream and the corn syrup in a small, heavy-bottomed saucepan. Cook over medium-high heat while continually stirring. Once the cream mixture comes to a rolling boil, pour directly over the chocolate and let it sit for 2 minutes. Stir, slowly incorporating all the ingredients, allowing the chocolate to fully melt. Using a candy thermometer placed in the center of the bowl, check the temperature. Once the ganache has reached 95°F (35°C), add the butter and stir well. Let the ganache sit for 45 minutes to an hour, or until it is firm enough to pipe. Line a baking sheet with parchment or waxed paper. Pipe or scoop the ganache as directed on page 83. Set aside to dry overnight. When ready, roll the ganache into smooth, round balls. Place on parchment paper and set aside.

2. To finish the truffles: Place the cocoa powder in a shallow bowl or casserole dish. Dip the truffles in the tempered chocolate one by one as directed on page 84. Immediately after dipping, roll each truffle in the cocoa powder until the truffle is fully covered. Let the chocolate fully set before removing the truffles from the cocoa powder.

Classic Milk 38 Percent

If you like the idea of pure chocolate and prefer milk chocolate to dark, then this is the truffle for you. Unencumbered by the addition of other flavors, it is smooth and creamy, with just enough of a chocolate profile to satisfy a craving.

This truffle is decorated by rolling it across a wire baking rack to add a spiky texture. This technique will give you an idea of how easy it is to use cooking equipment you probably already own to create unique and interesting textures and designs on your truffles. If you want to emphasize the chocolate a little bit more, simply roll the finished truffle in cocoa powder after dipping it in chocolate and omit the texture step. Or create your own unusual topping.

EASY   **Yield: 30 truffles**

6 ounces (167 g) 38 percent milk chocolate, chopped
2¾ ounces or ⅓ cup (77 g) heavy cream
¾ ounce or 1½ tablespoons (21 g) salted butter, cubed, soft but not melted

To finish truffles:
1 pound (453 g) 38 percent milk chocolate, tempered

---

1. To make the ganache: Place the chopped chocolate in a medium-size bowl. Set aside. Pour the heavy cream into a small, heavy-bottomed saucepan. Cook over medium-high heat while continually stirring. Once the cream comes to a rolling boil, pour directly over the chocolate and let sit for 2 minutes. Stir slowly to incorporate the cream, allowing the chocolate to fully melt. Using a candy thermometer placed in the center of the bowl, check the temperature. Once the ganache has reached 95°F (35°C), add the butter and stir well. Let the ganache sit 1 to 1½ hours, or until it is firm enough to pipe. Line a baking sheet with parchment or waxed paper. Pipe or scoop the ganache as directed on page 83. Set aside to dry overnight. When ready, roll the ganache into smooth, round balls. Place on parchment paper and set aside.

2. To finish the truffles: Dip the truffles in the tempered chocolate one by one as directed on page 84. Immediately after dipping, roll each truffle over a wire baking rack. Use a dipping fork or regular fork to roll the truffle around on the rack, creating a rough texture. Place on clean sheet of parchment paper and allow chocolate to fully set before removing.

Tip:

When making ganache, if the chocolate has not completely melted once it is fully incorporated with the hot liquid, place the mixture in the microwave for 1 to 5 seconds at a time, stirring after each time.

PISTACHIO-KIRSCH

Pistachios and cherries are a classic combination. You may have tried cherry truffles that hold an entire cherry, often macerated in liqueur, in their centers. My recipe is easier to make and the truffles still have a nice fruity flavor. If you want to boost that flavor, you can add a couple drops of natural cherry extract.

I like rolling these truffles in granulated pistachios for both the flavor and the crunch. Use the freshest pistachios you can find and, if possible, shell the nuts yourself. If you want to alter the recipe slightly, dip the truffles in white chocolate before coating them with the nuts. This will create a somewhat sweeter overall flavor.

EASY   **Yield: 30 truffles**

2 ounces (56 g) 64 percent bittersweet chocolate, chopped

3 ounces (84 g) 55 percent semisweet chocolate, chopped

3¼ ounces or 6½ tablespoons (91 g) heavy cream

¼ ounce or 1 teaspoon (7 g) light corn syrup

½ ounce or 1 tablespoon (14 g) salted butter, cubed, soft but not melted

½ ounce or 2 tablespoons (14 g) Kirsch

To finish truffles:

12 ounces (336 g) pistachios, shelled, lightly toasted, finely chopped

1 pound (453 g) 64 percent bittersweet chocolate, tempered

---

1. To make the ganache: Place the chopped chocolate in a medium-size bowl. Set aside. Combine the heavy cream and the corn syrup in a small, heavy-bottomed saucepan. Cook over medium-high heat while continually stirring. Once the cream mixture comes to a rolling boil, pour directly over the chocolate and let sit for 2 minutes. Stir, slowly incorporating all of the ingredients, allowing the chocolate to fully melt. Using a candy thermometer placed in the center of the bowl, check the temperature. Once the ganache has reached 95°F (35°C), add the butter and Kirsch, and stir well. Let the ganache sit for 30 minutes to 1 hour, or until it is firm enough to pipe. Line a baking sheet with parchment or waxed paper. Pipe or scoop the ganache as directed on page 83. Set aside to dry overnight. When ready, roll the ganache into smooth, round balls. Place on parchment paper and set aside.

2. To finish the truffles: Place the pistachios in a shallow bowl or casserole dish. Dip the truffles in the tempered chocolate one by one as directed on page 84. Immediately after dipping, roll each truffle in the pistachios until it is fully covered. Let the chocolate fully set before removing the truffles from the pistachios.

CANDY CANE

Candy canes are so quintessentially winter and remind everyone of their childhood. Rolling the truffles in candy cane pieces adds a pleasing crunch that contrasts nicely with their smooth truffle center.

How fresh the mint is when you buy it will dictate to some extent how strong the mint flavor of the final piece will be. If you can't find candy canes or are afraid they will make the truffles too minty, simply finish the truffles by rolling them in white chocolate and adding a texture design (as discussed on page 87). Likewise, if you prefer the candy cane crunch to the minty center, simply omit the mint flavoring and make a white chocolate ganache dipped in white chocolate and rolled in the candy cane pieces.

EASY   **Yield: 30 truffles**

6½ ounces (182 g) 29 percent white chocolate, chopped
2½ ounces or ⅓ cup minus 1 teaspoon (70 g) heavy cream
3 sprigs fresh mint
1/16 teaspoon or a splash (2 g) clear crème de menthe
2 to 4 drops natural peppermint oil
½ ounce or 1 tablespoon (14 g) salted butter, cubed, soft but not melted

To finish truffles:
12 ounces or 3 cups (336 g) candy cane pieces, roughly chopped
1 pound (453 g) 29 percent white chocolate, tempered

---

1. To make the ganache: Place the chopped chocolate in a medium-size bowl. Set aside. Combine the heavy cream and the fresh mint in a small, heavy-bottomed saucepan. Cook over medium-high heat until the cream mixture starts to simmer, then remove from heat and cover. Let the cream mixture steep for 15 minutes, then place the saucepan back on the stove, add the crème de menthe and the peppermint oil, and cook over medium-high heat. Once the cream mixture reaches a rolling boil, pour through a fine-mesh sieve directly over the chocolate. Let sit for 2 minutes. Stir, slowly incorporating all the ingredients. Using a candy thermometer placed in the center of the bowl, check the temperature. Once the ganache has reached 95°F (35°C), add the butter and stir well. Let the ganache sit for 30 minutes to 1 hour, or until it is firm enough to pipe. Line a baking sheet with parchment or waxed paper. Pipe or scoop the ganache as directed on page 83. Set aside to dry overnight. When ready, roll the ganache into smooth, round balls. Place on parchment paper and set aside.

2. To finish the truffles: Place the chopped candy canes in a shallow bowl or casserole dish. Dip the truffles in the tempered chocolate one by one as directed on page 84. Immediately after dipping, roll each truffle in the candy cane pieces until it is fully covered. Let the chocolate fully set before removing the truffles from the candy cane pieces.

Lemongrass–Coconut

The combination of fresh lemongrass and coconut imparts a very tropical feel to this truffle. The lemongrass flavor is quite pronounced yet finishes nicely with the toasted coconut. Both milk and dark chocolates provide a worthy background, and the white chocolate shell is just sweet enough to balance both flavors. The Mojito-flavored liqueur adds a little something extra to make all the flavors pop. If you cannot find this liqueur, rum will work just as nicely.

EASY **Yield: 30 truffles**

5½ ounces (154 g) 38 percent milk chocolate, chopped

¾ ounce (21 g) 64 percent bittersweet chocolate, chopped

1¾ ounces or 3½ tablespoons (49 g) heavy cream

1 ounce or 2 tablespoons (28 g) coconut milk

1 thick stalk (4" [10 cm] long) fresh lemongrass, chopped

¼ ounce or 1 teaspoon (7 g) light corn syrup

¼ ounce or 1½ teaspoons (7 g) salted butter, cubed, soft but not melted

¼ ounce or full 1 tablespoon (7 g) Mojito-flavored liqueur

To finish truffles:

6¼ ounces or 2 cups (175 g) shredded coconut, toasted

1 pound (453 g) 31 percent white chocolate, tempered

---

1. To make the ganache: Place the chopped chocolates in a medium-size bowl. Set aside. Combine the heavy cream, coconut milk, and lemongrass in a small, heavy-bottomed saucepan. Cook over medium-high heat until the mixture starts to simmer, then remove from heat and cover. Let steep for 15 minutes. Place the saucepan back on the stove, add the corn syrup, and cook over medium-high heat. Once the mixture reaches a rolling boil, pour through a fine-mesh sieve directly over the chocolate. Let sit for 2 minutes. Stir, slowly incorporating all the ingredients. Using a candy thermometer placed in the center of the bowl, check the temperature. Once the ganache has reached 95°F (35°C), add the butter and liqueur, and stir well. Let the ganache sit for 45 minutes to 1 hour, or until it is firm enough to pipe. Line a baking sheet with parchment or waxed paper. Pipe or scoop as directed on page 83. Set aside to dry overnight. When ready, roll the ganache into smooth, round balls. Place on parchment paper and set aside.

2. To finish the truffles: Place the toasted coconut in a shallow bowl or casserole dish. Dip the truffles in the tempered chocolate one by one as directed on page 84. Immediately after dipping, roll each truffle in the coconut until it is fully covered. Let the chocolate fully set before removing the truffles from the coconut.

SESAME

I recently began to incorporate sesame into my chocolates. I was pleasantly surprised at first to learn how well sesame blends with chocolate and how versatile a flavoring it is. Try to use a good-quality sesame oil with a strong sesame flavor, as this will dictate the flavor profile of the ganache.

As with other recipes in this chapter, I have followed through on the flavor to the design. And while I chose to only coat half the truffle with the sesame seeds, you might opt to cover the entire piece.

If you can only find one color seed, don't worry—that will not affect the overall taste. I like to use both ivory and black seeds for the color contrast.

EASY   **Yield: 30 truffles**

6 ounces (168 g) 38 percent milk chocolate, chopped
2¾ ounces or ⅓ cup (77 g) heavy cream
¼ ounce or 1 tablespoon (7 g) sesame oil
1 ounce or 2 tablespoons (28 g) salted butter, cubed, soft but not melted

To finish truffles:
6¾ ounces or 1⅓ cups (190 g) sesame seeds, a mixture of ivory and black
1 pound (453 g) 29 percent white chocolate, tempered

---

1. To make the ganache: Place the chocolate in a medium-size bowl. Set aside. Combine the heavy cream and sesame oil in a small, heavy-bottomed saucepan. Cook over medium-high heat while continually stirring. Once the cream mixture comes to a rolling boil, pour directly over the chocolate and let sit for 2 minutes. Stir, slowly incorporating all the ingredients. Using a candy thermometer placed in the center of the bowl, check the temperature. Once the ganache has reached 95°F (35°C), add the butter and stir well. Let the ganache sit for 2 hours, or until it is firm enough to pipe. Line a baking sheet with parchment or waxed paper. Pipe or scoop the ganache as directed on page 83. Set aside to dry overnight. When ready, roll the ganache into smooth, round balls. Place on parchment paper and set aside.

2. To finish the truffles: Preheat the oven to 350°F (180°C). Place the sesame seeds in a baking dish, stirring to evenly distribute the two colors of seeds. Lightly toast in the oven for 3 to 5 minutes, or until light brown. Once the seeds are toasted, remove from the oven and cool completely. Place the cooled seeds in a shallow bowl or casserole dish. Dip the truffles in the tempered chocolate one by one as directed on page 84. Immediately after dipping, drop each truffle into the toasted sesame seeds to only coat one side. Let the chocolate fully set before removing the truffles from the sesame seeds.

GINGERBREAD

This truffle is one of my favorites because it reminds me of being at home with family and friends. I have found that it is a crowd-pleaser among both kids and adults, so it's a great treat to bring to a party as a gift.

Using puffed rice cereal to finish the truffles is a bit unusual. This just goes to show you that garnishes can be found among the ingredients in your pantry as long as you use your imagination and are willing to experiment with new ideas. Use your favorite spice blend to customize the recipe.

EASY   **Yield: 30 truffles**

2 ounces (56 g) 64 percent bittersweet chocolate, chopped

2 ounces (56 g) 84 percent extra-bittersweet chocolate, chopped

¾ ounce (21 g) 38 percent milk chocolate, chopped

3¾ ounces or 7½ tablespoons (105 g) heavy cream

½ ounce or 2 teaspoons (14 g) light corn syrup

¼ ounce or 1½ teaspoons (7 g) salted butter, cubed, soft but not melted

¼ ounce or 3½ teaspoons (7 g) pumpkin pie spices

To finish truffles:

1 ounce or 1 cup (28 g) puffed rice cereal

¼ ounce or 3½ teaspoons (7 g) pumpkin pie spices

1 pound (453 g) 29 percent white chocolate, tempered

---

1. To make the ganache: Place the chopped chocolates in a medium-size bowl. Set aside. Combine the heavy cream and the corn syrup in a small, heavy-bottomed saucepan. Cook over medium-high heat while continually stirring. Once the cream mixture comes to a rolling boil, pour directly over the chocolate and let sit for 2 minutes. Stir, slowly incorporating all the ingredients, allowing the chocolate to fully melt. Using a candy thermometer placed in the center of the bowl, check the temperature. Once the ganache has reached 95°F (35°C), add the butter and spices and stir well. Let the ganache sit for 30 to 45 minutes, or until it is firm enough to pipe. Line a baking sheet with parchment or waxed paper. Pipe or scoop the ganache as directed on page 83. Set aside to dry overnight. When ready, roll the ganache into smooth, round balls. Place on parchment paper and set aside.

2. To finish the truffles: Preheat the oven to 350°F (180°C). Place the rice cereal and pumpkin pie spices in a baking dish, stirring to combine evenly. Lightly toast in the oven for 3 to 5 minutes. Once toasted, remove from the oven and cool. When cooled, pour the cereal mixture into a food processor, and pulse for a few seconds at a time to produce small granules. Do not overpulse or you will turn the mixture into a fine powder. Place in a shallow bowl or casserole dish and set aside. Dip the truffles in tempered chocolate one by one as directed on page 84. Immediately after dipping, roll each truffle in the cereal mixture until it is fully covered. Let the chocolate fully set before removing the truffles from the cereal mixture.

HONEY-THYME

Herbal and slightly floral in flavor, thyme is nicely balanced in this recipe by the addition of the honey. And while I prefer to use the Tasmanian honey listed in the recipe, you could actually use any honey you prefer. Keep in mind, however, that different honeys will impart different flavors that may or may not be complementary to the thyme.

To give these truffles a little more pizzazz, coat them with luster dust after adding an interesting texture. Luster dust is made from a natural, colored stone that is ground to a fine powder and is completely edible. If you like the way luster dust looks, feel free to use it to dust any of the truffles in this book!

EASY   **Yield: 30 truffles**

2½ ounces (70 g) 38 percent milk chocolate, chopped
2½ ounces (70 g) 64 percent bittersweet chocolate, chopped
1¼ ounces or 2½ tablespoons (35 g) heavy cream
3 sprigs fresh thyme
1¼ ounces or 2½ tablespoons (35 g) Tasmanian leatherwood honey
Pinch of salt

½ ounce (14 g) cocoa butter, melted
1½ ounces or 3 tablespoons (42 g) salted butter, cubed, soft but not melted.

To finish truffles:
1 pound (453 g) 38 percent milk chocolate, tempered
Luster dust, as needed

---

1. To make the ganache: Place the chocolate in a medium-size bowl. Set aside. Combine the heavy cream and the fresh thyme in a small, heavy-bottomed saucepan. Cook over medium-high heat until the cream starts to simmer, then remove from heat and cover. Let the mixture steep for 15 minutes. Strain through a fine-mesh sieve into a clean, small, heavy-bottomed saucepan and place back on the stove, add the honey and salt, and cook over medium-high heat. Once the cream reaches a rolling boil, pour directly over the chocolate. Let sit for 2 minutes. Stir, slowly incorporating all of the ingredients. Using a candy thermometer placed in the center of the bowl, check the temperature. Once the ganache has reached 95°F (35°C), add the cocoa butter and salted butter, and stir well. Let the ganache sit for

1 hour, or until it is firm enough to pipe. Line a baking sheet with parchment or waxed paper. Pipe or scoop the ganache as directed on page 83. Set aside to dry overnight. When ready, roll the ganache into smooth, round balls. Place on parchment paper and set aside.

2. To finish the truffles: Dip the truffles in tempered chocolate one by one as directed on page 84. Immediately after dipping, roll each truffle over a wire baking rack. Use a dipping fork or regular fork to roll the truffle around on the rack, creating a rough texture. Place on clean sheet of parchment paper and allow chocolate to set completely. Brush with luster dust before removing.

CARIBBEAN COCKTAIL

This truffle is meant to be a chocolate version of a tropical fruit drink. White chocolate forms the base of this ganache, for a sweet and creamy consistency. This ganache smells great while you are making the truffles and always makes me think of sitting on the beach drinking an ice-cold blender drink.

If you cannot find gold leaf to decorate your truffles, another great finish is to roll the truffle in toasted shredded coconut.

EASY   **Yield: 30 truffles**

5¾ ounces (161 g) 29 percent white chocolate, chopped
¾ ounce or 1½ tablespoons (21 g) heavy cream
¾ ounce or 1½ tablespoons (21 g) coconut milk
1 ounce or 2½ tablespoons (28 g) pineapple juice
½ ounce or 2 teaspoons (14 g) light corn syrup
¾ ounce or 1½ tablespoons (21 g) salted butter, cubed, soft but not melted
¼ ounce or 1 full tablespoon (7 g) good-quality dark rum, such as Myers

¼ ounce or full 1 tablespoon (7 g) Malibu rum
¾ ounce (21 g) candied pineapple, finely diced

To finish truffles:
1 pound (453 g) 38 percent milk chocolate, tempered
Edible gold leaf

---

1. To make the ganache: Place the chopped chocolate in a medium-size bowl. Set aside. Combine the heavy cream, coconut milk, pineapple juice, and corn syrup in a small, heavy-bottomed saucepan. Cook over medium-high heat while continually stirring. Once the mixture comes to a rolling boil, pour directly over the chocolate and let sit for 2 minutes. Stir, slowly incorporating all the ingredients, allowing the chocolate to fully melt. Using a candy thermometer placed in the center of the bowl, check the temperature. Once the ganache has reached 95°F (35°C), add the butter, rums, and candied pineapple, and stir well. Let the ganache sit for

1 to 1½ hours, until it is firm enough to pipe. Line a baking sheet with parchment or waxed paper. Pipe or scoop the ganache as directed on page 83. Set aside to dry overnight. When ready, roll the ganache into smooth, round balls. Place on parchment paper and set aside.

2. To finish the truffles: Dip the truffles in the tempered chocolate one by one as directed on page 84. Immediately after dipping, place on a clean sheet of parchment paper and allow chocolate to fully set. Once set, top each truffle with a piece of edible gold leaf.

SOUTH OF THE BORDER

This recipe calls for habanero oil, which offers more consistency then fresh peppers. If you have ever cut up fresh habaneros and then rubbed your eyes after washing your hands not quite well enough... Ay, chihuahua!

MEDIUM   **Yield: 30 truffles**

For pineapple purée:

1 pound (453 g) fresh pineapple, peeled and cubed

1½ ounces or 7 tablespoons (42 g) confectioners' sugar

For ganache:

5¼ ounces (147 g) 38 percent milk chocolate, chopped

¾ ounce (21 g) 64 percent bittersweet chocolate, chopped

2 ounces or ¼ cup (56 g) heavy cream

1 ounce or 3 tablespoons (28 g) pineapple purée

¼ ounce or 1 teaspoon (7 g) light corn syrup

¼ ounce or 1½ teaspoons (7 g) salted butter, cubed, soft but not melted

¼ ounce or full 1 tablespoon (7 g) Mojito-flavored liqueur

1/16 teaspoon or a splash (2 g) habanero oil

To finish truffles:

5¾ ounces (161 g) dried pineapple, finely diced

8 ounces or 1 cup (224 g) raw sugar

1 pound (453 g) 29 percent white chocolate, tempered

¼ ounce or 1½ teaspoons (7 g) chile powder

1. To make the pineapple purée: Place the pineapple cubes in the food processor and pulse until the fruit starts to liquefy. Add the confectioners' sugar and process the fruit on a low speed until completely liquid. Strain the purée through a fine-mesh sieve. Store in an airtight container in the refrigerator until needed.

2. To make the ganache: Place the chocolate in a medium-size bowl. Set aside. Combine the heavy cream, pineapple purée, and the corn syrup in a small, heavy-bottomed saucepan. Cook over medium-high heat while continually stirring. Once the mixture comes to a rolling boil, pour directly over the chocolate and let sit for 2 minutes. Stir, slowly incorporating all the ingredients, allowing the chocolate to fully melt. Using a candy thermometer placed in the center of the bowl, check the temperature. Once the ganache has reached 95°F (35°C), add the butter, liqueur, and habanero oil, and stir well. Let the ganache sit for 1½ hours, or until it is firm enough to pipe. Line a baking sheet with parchment or waxed paper. Pipe or scoop the ganache as directed on page 83. Set aside to dry overnight. When ready, roll the ganache into smooth, round balls. Place on parchment paper and set aside.

3. To finish the truffles: Combine the diced, dried pineapple and the sugar in a shallow bowl or casserole dish. Dip the truffles in the tempered chocolate one by one as directed on page 84. Immediately after dipping, roll the truffles in the dried fruit mixture. Place the truffles on a clean sheet of parchment paper and lightly sprinkle with chile powder. Allow chocolate to fully set before removing.

Banana Caramel

Instead of using a creamy caramel, this truffle contains crunchy caramel, ground up and added into the ganache for texture as well as flavor. If you are a caramel fan, another fun way to finish this truffle would be to make an extra batch of the caramel crunch, grind it up as directed, and use that to coat the dipped pieces. If making the caramel crunch presents too much of a challenge, don't worry, the truffles will still taste good without it.

DIFFICULT **Yield: 30 truffles**

For banana purée:

2 large, ripe bananas

¼ ounce or 1½ tablespoons (7 g) confectioners' sugar

For caramel crunch:

1 ounce or 2 tablespoons (28 g) granulated sugar

¼ ounce or 1 teaspoon (7 g) light corn syrup

For banana caramel ganache:

2¼ ounces (63 g) 29 percent white chocolate, chopped

1¼ ounces (35 g) 38 percent milk chocolate, chopped

¾ ounce or 1½ tablespoons (21 g) heavy cream

2¼ ounces or ⅓ cup (63 g) banana purée

1½ ounces (42 g) cocoa butter, melted and cooled

¼ ounce or 1½ teaspoons (7 g) salted butter, cubed, soft but not melted

¼ ounce or full 1 tablespoon (7 g) good-quality dark rum, such as Myers

½ teaspoon or a splash (2 g) vanilla extract

To finish truffles:

4 ounces or full 1 cup (112 g) cocoa powder

4 ounces or 1 cup plus 2 tablespoons (112 g) confectioners' sugar

1 pound (453 g) 38 percent milk chocolate, tempered

---

1. To make the banana purée: Peel the bananas and place in food processor. Add the confectioners' sugar and pulse until the bananas liquefy. Strain through a fine-mesh sieve into a clean bowl. Cover tightly with plastic wrap and refrigerate until ready to use.

2. To make the caramel crunch: Place one Silpat right side up on a heat-resistant counter-top or table. Set aside the second Silpat, along with a rolling pin. Combine the granulated sugar and corn syrup in a small, heavy-bottomed saucepan and place over medium-high heat. Do not stir. Cook until the mixture reaches a medium amber color. Immediately and carefully pour the hot sugar mixture onto the first Silpat. Place the second Silpat on top of the first, and gently and carefully roll flat using a rolling pin. Set aside for 10 to 20 minutes to cool. Peel off the top Silpat, break up the sugar into shards, and place in a food processor. Pulse the shards into a coarse powder. Set aside until ready to use.

3. To make the ganache: Place the chopped chocolates in a medium-size bowl. Set aside. Combine the heavy cream and banana purée in a small, heavy-bottomed saucepan. Cook over medium-high heat while continually stirring. Once the mixture comes to a rolling boil, pour directly over the chocolate and let sit for 2 minutes. Stir, slowly incorporating all of the ingredients, allowing the chocolate to fully melt. Using a candy thermometer placed in the center of the bowl, check the temperature. Once the ganache has reached 95°F (35°C), add the cocoa butter, butter, rum, and vanilla extract, and stir well. Fold in the ground caramel. Let the ganache sit for 1 hour and 15 minutes, or until it is firm enough to

pipe. Line a baking sheet with parchment or waxed paper. Pipe or scoop the ganache as directed on page 83. Set aside to dry overnight. When ready, roll the ganache into smooth, round balls. Place on parchment paper and set aside.

4. To finish the truffles: Combine the cocoa powder and confectioners' sugar in a shallow bowl or casserole dish. Dip the truffles in the tempered chocolate one by one as directed on page 84. Immediately after dipping, roll each truffle in the cocoa mixture until it is fully covered. Let the chocolate fully set before removing the truffles from the cocoa mixture.

PEANUT BUTTER SIZZLE

Okay, so a peanut butter truffle may not seem like a daring flavor. But have you ever tried peanut butter with cayenne pepper? The pepper brings the peanut butter to a whole other dimension!

It's actually quite interesting how well these two flavors work together. The cayenne seems to bring out the nuttiness of the peanuts, and the creaminess of the peanut butter cuts the bite of the cayenne.

When you eat these truffles, you may not notice the heat at first. You will probably just taste the peanut butter flavor. And then, suddenly, the cayenne will creep up and there will be a slight heat at the back of your throat.

If making the caramel crunch presents too much of a challenge, don't worry. The truffles will still taste good without it.

DIFFICULT   **Yield: 30 truffles**

For caramel crunch:
³⁄₄ ounce or 4¹⁄₂ teaspoons (21 g) granulated sugar
¹⁄₄ ounce or 1 teaspoon (7 g) light corn syrup

For peanut butter ganache:
3¹⁄₄ ounces (91 g) 38 percent milk chocolate, chopped

4³⁄₄ ounces or ¹⁄₂ cup (133 g) creamy peanut butter
¹⁄₄ ounce (7 g) cocoa butter, melted and cooled
Pinch ground cayenne pepper

To finish truffles:
8¹⁄₂ ounces (238 g) Spanish peanuts, skin removed
1 pound (453 g) 61 percent bittersweet chocolate, tempered

---

1. To make the caramel crunch: Place one Silpat right side up on a heat-resistant counter-top or table. Combine the granulated sugar and corn syrup in a small, heavy-bottomed saucepan and place over medium-high heat. Do not stir. Cook until the mixture reaches a medium amber color. Immediately and carefully pour the hot sugar mixture onto the first Silpat. Place the second Silpat on top of the first, and gently and carefully roll flat using a rolling pin. Set aside for 10 to 20 minutes to cool. Peel off the top Silpat, break up the sugar into shards, and place in a food processor. Pulse the shards into a coarse powder. Set aside until ready to use.

2. To make the ganache: Place the chocolate into a medium-size microwaveable bowl. Melt in the microwave at 50 percent power for 15 to 20 seconds at a time, stirring between heatings. Once the milk chocolate has started to melt, use a candy thermometer placed in the center of the bowl to check the temperature. Once the chocolate has reached 88°F (31°C), combine with the peanut butter. Stir in the cocoa butter, cayenne pepper, and caramel crunch. Stirring occasionally, let the ganache sit for 1 hour, or until it is firm enough to pipe. Line a baking sheet with parchment or waxed paper Pipe or scoop the ganache as directed on page 83.

Set aside to dry overnight. When ready, roll the ganache into smooth, round balls. Place on parchment paper and set aside.

3. To finish the truffles: Preheat the oven to 350°F (180°C). Grind the peanuts to a mealy consistency in a food processor. Toast the granulated peanuts in the oven for 5 to 7 minutes, or until golden brown. When completely cooled, place the granulated peanuts in a shallow bowl or casserole dish. Dip the truffles in the tempered chocolate one by one as directed on page 84. Immediately after dipping, roll each truffle in the granulated peanuts until it is fully covered. Let the chocolate fully set before removing the truffles from the granulated peanuts.

Chapter Six

MOLDED CHOCOLATES

M olded chocolates are what most people envision when they think of chocolates found inside boxed sets. These chocolates come in myriad shapes, sizes, and fillings. Traditional molded pieces are generally coated in pure milk, white, or dark chocolate. Modern molded chocolates often incorporate colored cocoa butter airbrushed onto the piece before or after the molding process, for a more interesting appearance. A step above truffles, molded chocolates require a slightly higher skill level and more specialized equipment.

This chapter will go through the techniques and equipment needed to make your own molded masterpieces. As with the truffle recipes, use these as a guide to invent your own. The appearance of any of the resulting chocolates can be enhanced by applying the airbrush or painting techniques covered in this chapter. However, if you find that step too challenging, simply use tempered chocolate for molding your pieces. Although technically you could substitute a different type of chocolate for the one used in each recipe for the molded shell, keep in mind the overall balance of sweetness and flavor of the finished piece before you do so. A piece whose filling is molded in a dark chocolate shell will have a different taste when molded in white chocolate.

What You Will Need to Get Started

Chocolate and candy molds are generally easy to find, at either a local candy-making supply store or an arts-and-crafts store such as Michael's. When buying a chocolate mold, keep in mind its use and quality. If you are only going to use the mold one or two times, then you might want to purchase an inexpensive one. Made of thin plastic, these molds are very flexible and break easily. They are generally considered disposable

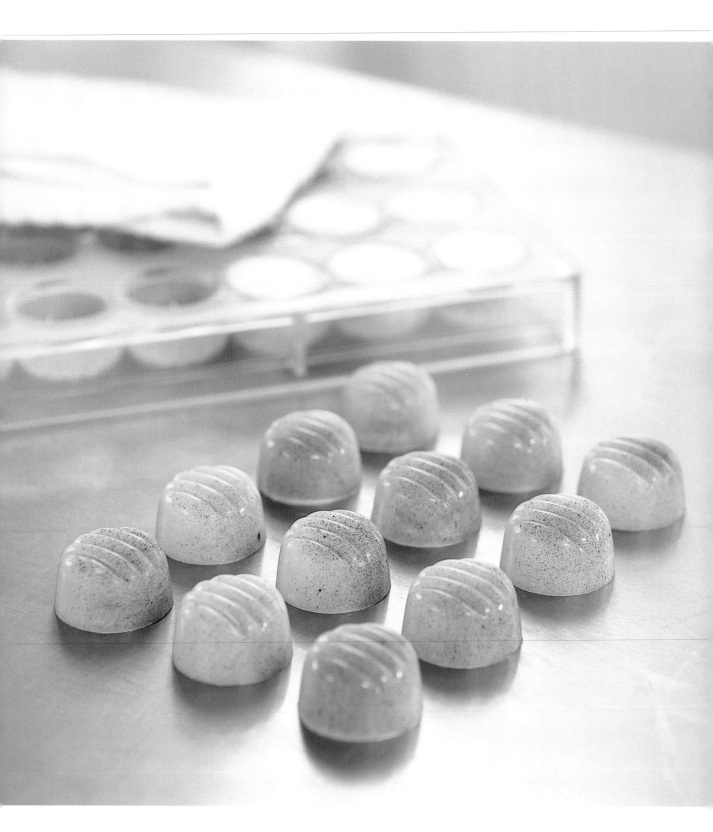

as they are not long-lasting. However, they are also not very costly, so they are a good option for someone just starting out and not ready to commit to more permanent molds.

Professional chocolate makers generally use heavy-duty polycarbonate molds. These molds are hard, solid, and made to withstand multiple uses over a long period of time. However, they can be quite expensive, especially for the novice chocolatier.

No matter what type of mold you choose, you will need to take care of it. Most important, make sure to never scratch the inside of the mold, the part that comes into contact with the tempered chocolate. A very sensitive medium, chocolate will pick up any imperfection in the mold. These imperfections will show up on the surface of your candies. Once the inside of a mold is scratched, it is basically useless.

When dirty, molds should be gently cleaned in warm soapy water and rubbed with a very soft sponge, nothing abrasive. To dry a mold, set it upside down on a wire baking rack, allowing air to circulate under and around it. When dry, buff the inside of the mold gently with soft cotton balls.

Fillings and Flavors

Molded chocolates offer more flexibility with fillings than truffles do. Aside from ganache fillings, molded chocolates may contain nut pastes, jam layers, and liquid centers, as the surrounding hard chocolate shell offers more protection. Molded chocolates are different than truffles in that their shells are created first and then filled with their centers. While many molded pieces today showcase more interesting flavors, they still seem to only contain one layer of filling. If you are the adventurous type, don't let this limit your imagination. Once you feel comfortable making molded chocolates, experiment by adding different layers in each piece.

When making fillings for molded chocolates, keep in mind that the ganache recipes used in the truffle chapter will not necessarily work here. Truffle ganache contains 30 percent less heavy cream than does ganache for molded chocolate. If you put a truffle ganache into a molded piece, the center would be very thick and dry in comparison with a correctly balanced recipe. Finally, if you decide to make one of the recipes in this chapter but want to change the chocolate used for its molded shell, just remember to consider the overall balance of the piece when doing so. White chocolate is much sweeter than dark chocolate, for example.

TIP:

When tasting molded chocolates, pay close attention to the thickness of their shells. The mark of a job well done is a thin, even, shiny shell with a nice snap and crunch when eaten.

How To Mold Chocolates

Making molded chocolates starts with creating the outer shell. Then the filling is put in and allowed to set, and the molds are closed to keep the fillings inside. To make a shell, you will need tempered chocolate. Start with a large, wide bowl filled with tempered chocolate. It's much easier to fill molds if you have prepared more chocolate than is actually needed, so temper a large amount.

2. Use a ladle to completely fill the mold with tempered chocolate. Shake the mold around a little to ensure that the tempered chocolate coats every surface of the mold cavities.

3. Turn the filled mold over the bowl of chocolate allowing any excess chocolate to drip out. Lightly tap the mold with the back of a heavy knife or spatula to help remove the excess chocolate. Lay the mold upside down on a parchment paper-lined baking sheet. After a few minutes check the sides of the mold cavities to see if the chocolate has begun to set.

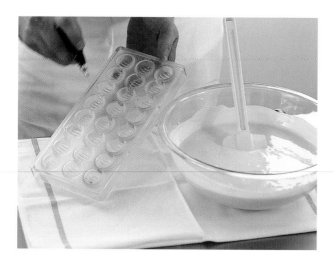

1. To airbrush or paint inside the mold before adding the chocolate, simply apply the airbrush in the desired pattern or paint the appropriate brushstrokes into the mold. Allow this to almost set before adding the chocolate. For a finished piece: airbrush or paint your pattern and then allow to set.

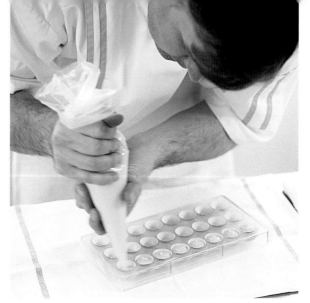

4. Once it has begun to thicken and set, use the blade of a chef's knife to scrape the top of the mold clean. Return the mold to the baking sheet and allow it to finish setting completely before adding the filling.

5. Add the filling and allow it to set. Next, ladle tempered chocolate over the top of the mold.

6. Scrape off the excess to create what will actually be the bottom of the molded chocolate. This thin layer of chocolate is then allowed to harden before the molds are inverted and lightly tapped to remove the finished molded chocolates.

To Finish the Molded Chocolates

Ladle approximately 4 to 8 ounces of tempered chocolate onto the top of the filled shells. Using a large offset spatula, spread the chocolate evenly across the top of the mold, making sure to completely cover the entire surface. Scrape off any excess chocolate into the bowl. Put the mold in the refrigerator for 10 to 15 minutes, or until the chocolate has released from the sides of the mold. Remove from the refrigerator and allow the chocolates to come to room temperature before unmolding. Remove the chocolates by inverting the mold over a sheet of parchment paper and gently tapping the mold against the counter to release the chocolates, allowing them to drop onto the sheet of paper.

FENNEL

While it may seem unusual, using fennel is similar to using licorice or anise. Because the fennel flavor is quite subtle, it makes sense to use white chocolate as its sweetness and creamy texture further enhances the overall enjoyment of this piece.

EASY   **Yield: 28 chocolates**

For chocolate shells:

2 pounds (906 g) 29 percent white chocolate, tempered

For fennel ganache:

6¼ ounces (175 g) 29 percent white chocolate, chopped

3½ ounces or ½ cup minus 1 tablespoon (98 g) heavy cream

½ bulb fresh fennel, trimmed, seeded, and chopped

½ ounce or 1 tablespoon (14 g) salted butter, cubed, soft but not melted

¼ ounce (7 g) cocoa butter, melted and cooled to body temperature

¼ ounce or full 1 tablespoon (7 g) Marie Brizard Anisette or other licorice-flavored liqueur

To finish chocolates:

8 ounces (224 g) 29 percent white chocolate, tempered

---

1. To prepare the molded shells: Mold the chocolate shells according to the procedure on page 108. Set aside until the chocolate has completely set and the shells are ready to be filled.

2. To make the ganache: Place the chopped chocolate in a medium-size bowl. Pour the heavy cream and fennel into a small, heavy-bottomed saucepan. Cook over medium-high heat until the cream mixture begins to simmer. Remove from heat, cover, and allow the fennel to steep for 45 minutes. After steeping, pour the cream through a fine-mesh sieve into a clean bowl or glass measuring cup. Measure or weigh out 2¾ ounces or ⅓ cup (75 g) fennel-infused cream and pour into a clean, small, heavy-bottomed saucepan. (If there is not enough of the fennel infusion, add enough fresh cream to make up required amount.

If there is too much infusion, discard the extra.) Cook over medium-high heat until the cream mixture comes to a rapid boil. Remove from heat and pour directly over the white chocolate. Let sit for 2 minutes. Slowly stir to incorporate. Using a candy thermometer placed in the center of the bowl, check the temperature. Once the ganache has reached 95°F (35°C), add the butter, cocoa butter, and Anisette, and mix to combine. Pour the ganache into a piping bag or large sandwich bag. Cut a corner from the bag to create a small opening. Pipe the ganache into the molded shells, filling each mold cavity three-quarters full. Gently tap the filled molds against the counter or table to release any trapped air bubbles. Let the ganache sit overnight at room temperature to dry.

3. To finish the molded chocolates: see page 109.

LIME–PASTIS

This combination is based on a sorbet I had while vacationing in Mexico. The sorbet was actually meant to be a palate cleanser and was served in between courses at dinner. I found the intense fresh citrus flavor of the lime and the sweetness of the Pastis liqueur to be quite interesting and thought the same combination would translate well into chocolate.

Pastis is a licorice-tasting liqueur and its essence, more than its actual flavor, is what follows as you finish eating the chocolate.

EASY   **Yield: 28 chocolates**

For chocolate shells:
2 pounds (906 g) 38 percent milk chocolate, tempered

For lime ganache:
5 3/4 ounces (161 g) 38 percent milk chocolate, chopped
3/4 ounce (21 g) 64 percent bittersweet chocolate, chopped
2 ounces or 1/4 cup (56 g) heavy cream
Juice of 1 lime

Zest of 1 lime
1/4 ounce or 1 teaspoon (7 g) light corn syrup
1/4 ounce or 1 1/2 teaspoons (7 g) salted butter, cubed, soft but not melted
1/4 ounce or full 1 tablespoon (7 g) Pastis or other licorice-flavored liqueur
2 to 4 drops natural lime oil

To finish chocolates:
8 ounces (224 g) 38 percent milk chocolate, tempered

---

1. To prepare the molded shells: Mold the chocolate shells according to the procedure on page 108. Set aside until the chocolate has completely set and the shells are ready to be filled.

2. To make the ganache: Combine the chopped chocolates in a medium-size bowl. Pour the cream into a small, heavy-bottomed saucepan and add the lime juice, lime zest, and corn syrup. Cook the cream over medium-high heat until it reaches a rolling boil. Immediately pour through a fine-mesh sieve onto the chopped chocolate. Let sit for 2 minutes to melt the chocolate. Stir slowly to incorporate. Using a

candy thermometer placed in the center of the bowl, check the temperature. Once the ganache has reached 95°F (35°C), add the butter, Pastis, and lime oil, and mix to combine. Pour the ganache into a piping bag or large sandwich bag. Cut a corner from the bag to create a small opening. Pipe the ganache into the molded shells, filling each shell three-quarters full. Gently tap the filled shells against the counter or table to release any trapped air bubbles. Let the ganache sit overnight at room temperature to dry.

3. To finish the molded chocolates: see page 109.

MANGO-MINT-CORIANDER

When I create a new chocolate collection, I try to base it around the flavors of the season in which the collection will be offered. Mango is a winter flavor and one that pairs well with chocolate. When I was looking for an interesting way to use mango, it occurred to me that ground coriander might be a nice accompaniment. I added fresh mint to the mix to bring in a clean, slightly peppery nuance that was at the same time floral, and therefore synergistic with the mango and coriander.

EASY   **Yield: 28 chocolates**

For chocolate shells:
2 pounds (906 g) 64 percent bittersweet chocolate, tempered

For mango-mint-coriander ganache:
5¼ ounces (147 g) 38 percent milk chocolate, chopped
½ ounce (14 g) 64 percent bittersweet chocolate, chopped
2 ounces or ¼ cup (56 g) heavy cream
3 sprigs fresh mint

1¼ ounces or 2 tablespoons (35 g) mango purée
¼ ounce or 1 teaspoon (7 g) light corn syrup
¼ ounce or 1½ teaspoons (7 g) salted butter, cubed, soft but not melted
⅛ ounce or 1½ teaspoons (3.5 g) clear crème de menthe
Pinch ground coriander

To finish chocolates:
8 ounces (224 g) 64 percent bittersweet chocolate, tempered

---

1. To prepare the molded shells: Mold the chocolate shells according to the procedure on page 108. Set aside until the chocolate has completely set and the shells are ready to be filled.

2. To make the ganache: Place the chopped chocolates in a medium-size bowl. Pour the cream into a small, heavy-bottomed saucepan and add the fresh mint. Cook the cream mixture over medium-high heat until it begins to simmer. Remove from heat, cover the saucepan, and let steep for 10 minutes. Strain through a fine-mesh sieve into a clean, medium-size saucepan. Add the mango purée and corn syrup, and return the saucepan to the stove, uncovered. Cook over medium-high heat until the cream mixture reaches

a rolling boil. Pour onto the chopped chocolate. Let sit for 2 minutes to melt the chocolate. Stir slowly to incorporate. Using a candy thermometer placed in the center of the bowl, check the temperature. Once the ganache has reached 95°F (35°C), add the butter, crème de menthe, and ground coriander, and mix to combine. Pour the ganache into a piping bag or large sandwich bag. Cut a corner from the bag to create a small opening. Pipe the ganache into the molded shells, filling each shell three-quarters full. Gently tap the filled shells against the counter or table to release any trapped air bubbles. Let the ganache sit overnight at room temperature to dry.

3. To finish the molded chocolates: see page 109.

RED ROSE

Red rose is a traditional raspberry filling with rose oil added for a slightly different flavor variation. I was hesitant at first to use rose oil, which can be overbearing in both smell and taste if misused. However, when it is used in moderation, one is almost unaware of its presence. When you try this chocolate you will first and foremost taste the raspberry. The rose flavor will come with the finish. You'll notice the perfume lingers long after you have swallowed the last bite.

EASY   **Yield: 28 chocolates**

For chocolate shells:
2 pounds (906 g) 64 percent bittersweet chocolate, tempered

For red rose ganache:
5¼ ounces (147 g) 64 percent bittersweet chocolate, chopped
1½ ounces or 3 tablespoons (42 g) heavy cream
½ ounce or 2 teaspoons (14 g) light corn syrup
1½ ounces or ¼ cup (42 g) raspberry purée

½ ounce or 1 tablespoon (14 g) granulated sugar
½ ounce or 1 tablespoon (14 g) salted butter, cubed, soft but not melted
2 to 4 drops culinary-grade rose petal oil or rose water

To finish chocolates:
8 ounces (224 g) 64 percent bittersweet chocolate, tempered

1. To prepare the molded shells: Mold the chocolate shells according to the procedure on page 108. Set aside until the chocolate has completely set and the shells are ready to be filled.

2. To make the ganache: Place the chopped chocolate in a medium-size bowl. Pour the cream into a small, heavy-bottomed saucepan and add the corn syrup, raspberry purée, and sugar. Stirring constantly, cook over medium-high heat until the cream mixture reaches a rolling boil. Pour onto the chopped chocolate. Let the ganache sit for 2 minutes to melt the chocolate. Stir slowly to incorporate. Using a candy thermometer placed in the center of the bowl, check the temperature. Once the ganache has reached 95°F (35°C), add the butter and rose oil, and mix to combine. Pour the ganache into a piping bag or large sandwich bag. Cut a corner from the bag to create a small opening. Pipe the ganache into the molded shells, filling each shell three-quarters full. Gently tap the filled shells against the counter or table to release any trapped air bubbles. Let the ganache sit overnight at room temperature to dry.

3. To finish the molded chocolates: see page 109.

VANILLA

Packed with fresh vanilla bean seeds in a pure white chocolate ganache, this piece is sweet, creamy, and fragrant.

Vanilla beans can be quite pricey and good ones are often hard to find. But they are worth it if you can get them. Look for beans that are plump and moist, as those will contain the most flavorful seeds. Stay away from beans that seem to be dried out and brittle. If you cannot find fresh vanilla beans, use the best pure vanilla extract you can find.

EASY   **Yield: 28 chocolates**

For chocolate shells:
2 pounds (906 g) 29 percent white chocolate, tempered

For vanilla ganache:
6½ ounces (182 g) 29 percent white chocolate, chopped
2¾ ounces or ⅓ cup (77 g) heavy cream

2 vanilla beans, split and scraped
¾ ounce or 1½ tablespoons (21 g) salted butter, cubed, soft but not melted

To finish chocolates:
8 ounces (224 g) 29 percent white chocolate, tempered

1. To prepare the molded shells: Mold the chocolate shells according to the procedure on page 108. Set aside until the chocolate has completely set and the shells are ready to be filled.

2. To make the ganache: Place the chopped chocolate in a medium-size bowl. Pour the cream into a small, heavy-bottomed saucepan and add the vanilla bean seeds. Cook the cream mixture over medium-high heat until it begins to simmer. Remove from heat, cover the saucepan, and let steep for 15 minutes. Return the saucepan to the stove, uncovered, and cook over medium-high heat until the cream mixture reaches a rolling boil. Immediately pour through a fine-mesh sieve onto the chopped chocolate.

Let the ganache sit for 2 minutes to melt the chocolate. Stir slowly to incorporate. Using a candy thermometer placed in the center of the bowl, check the temperature. Once the ganache has reached 95°F (35°C), add the butter and mix to combine. Pour the ganache into a piping bag or large sandwich bag. Cut a corner from the bag to create a small opening. Pipe the ganache into the molded shells, filling each shell three-quarters full. Gently tap the filled shells against the counter or table to release any trapped air bubbles. Let the ganache sit overnight at room temperature to dry.

3. To finish the molded chocolates: see page 109.

Hazelnut Praline

Hazelnut praline is one of those classic flavors that never goes out of style. If you have tried praline centers in the past, you should notice a difference when you make these. Homemade praline is much more flavorful and moist because it is made fresh.

It is imperative that you use fresh nuts or your praline will taste rancid, so buy the nuts from a reputable vendor. And be sure to toast the nuts to bring out their full flavor. Pralines made with raw nuts taste thin and one-dimensional.

This recipe calls for cocoa butter. The addition of this ingredient helps to keep the ganache fluid and ensures a good mouth-feel. Without it, the ganache would have more of a peanut butter consistency, thick and sticky.

MEDIUM   Yield: 28 chocolates

For chocolate shells:
2 pounds (906 g) 64 percent bittersweet chocolate, tempered

For hazelnut praline:
3½ ounces (98 g) whole hazelnuts, skin removed, toasted
7 ounces or ¾ cup plus 2 tablespoons (196 g) granulated sugar
¾ ounce or 1½ tablespoons (21 g) water

For hazelnut praline ganache:
3¼ ounces (91 g) 38 percent milk chocolate, melted and warmed to 95°F (35°C)
7 ounces or ¾ cup (196 g) hazelnut praline, warmed to 95°F (35°C)
¼ ounce (7 g) cocoa butter, melted and warmed to 95°F (35°C)

To finish chocolates:
8 ounces (224 g) 64 percent bittersweet chocolate, tempered

---

1. To prepare the molded shells: Mold the chocolate shells according to the procedure on page 108. Set aside until the chocolate has completely set and the shells are ready to be filled.

2. To make the hazelnut praline: Place the toasted hazelnuts on a baking sheet lined with a Silpat and set aside. Combine the sugar and water in a small, heavy-bottomed saucepan and cook over high heat. Do not stir the sugar. If the edges start to burn, swirl the pot around a few times to coat the sides of the pan with water, and place pan back on the heat. Cook the sugar to a smoking dark amber caramel. Remove from heat and carefully pour directly over the hazelnuts. Let cool completely. Break the sugar and hazelnuts into pieces and put in a food processor. Grind to a pasty liquid consistency, making sure no large hazelnut chunks remain. This should take 5 to 10 minutes of processing. Store the hazelnut praline in the refrigerator in an airtight container until ready to use. Hazelnut praline can also be stored in the freezer for a longer period of time. Thaw in the refrigerator overnight prior to using.

3. To make the ganache: Combine the warmed chocolate and hazelnut praline until fully incorporated. Add the cocoa butter and stir well. Pour the ganache into a piping bag or large sandwich bag. Cut a corner from the bag to create a small opening. Pipe the ganache into the molded shells, filling each shell three-quarters full. Gently tap the filled shells against the counter or table to release any trapped air bubbles. Let the ganache sit overnight at room temperature to dry.

4. To finish the molded chocolates: see page 109.

CINNAMON–HAZELNUT

This chocolate is different from the classic hazelnut praline because of the addition of cinnamon. When one thinks of premium chocolate candies, European chocolates generally come to mind. And cinnamon is so not a European flavor! In fact, it is quintessentially American. Hazelnuts, too, are very American. The state of Oregon in particular is known for its hazelnut production. So I decided it would be nice to mix these two great American products together and, voilà, here we have it.

If you are a true cinnamon fan, use more cinnamon sticks to increase the cinnamon flavor. When you buy cinnamon sticks, try to get them from a vendor who turns his product over frequently, to ensure you are getting the freshest cinnamon possible.

MEDIUM **Yield: 28 chocolates**

For chocolate shells:
2 pounds (906 g) 38 percent milk chocolate, tempered

For hazelnut purée:
3½ ounces (98 g) whole hazelnuts, skin removed
3½ ounces (98 g) whole hazelnuts, skin on

For cinnamon ganache:
5½ ounces (154 g) 38 percent milk chocolate, chopped
3 ounces or ⅓ cup plus 1 tablespoon (84 g) heavy cream
2 cinnamon sticks

³⁄₈ ounce or 3¼ teaspoons (14 g) hazelnut purée, room temperature
¾ ounce or 1½ tablespoons (21 g) salted butter, cubed, soft but not melted
¼ ounce or 2 teaspoons (7 g) ground cinnamon

To finish chocolates:
8 ounces (224 g) 38 percent milk chocolate, tempered

---

1. To prepare the molded shells: Mold the chocolate shells according to procedure on page 108. Set aside until the chocolate has completely set and the shells are ready to be filled.

2. To make the hazelnut purée: Preheat the oven to 350°F (180°C). Spread the nuts on a baking sheet and place in the preheated oven. Cook until the nuts are fully toasted in the center. To test for doneness, remove one nut from the oven and cut it in half. The center should be a golden brown at the very core. Remove from the oven and allow to cool completely. When cool, place the nuts in a food processor and process on a low speed to a pastelike consistency. Use a rubber spatula to scrape around the inside of the food processor and near the blade. Store the hazelnut purée in the refrigerator in an airtight container until ready to use. Hazelnut purée can also be stored in the freezer for a longer period of time. Thaw in the refrigerator overnight prior to using.

3. To make the ganache: Place the chopped chocolate in a medium-size bowl. Pour the cream into a small, heavy-bottomed saucepan and add cinnamon sticks. Cook the cream over medium-high heat until it begins to simmer. Remove from heat, cover the saucepan, and let the cream and cinnamon steep for 30 minutes. Strain mixture through a fine-mesh sieve into a clean medium-size saucepan and return to the stove, uncovered. Cook over medium-high heat until the cream reaches a rolling boil. Pour the cream onto the chopped chocolate and let sit for 2 minutes to melt the chocolate. Slowly stir to incorporate. Using a candy thermometer placed in the center of the bowl, check the temperature. Once the ganache has reached 95°F (35°C), add the hazelnut purée, butter, and ground cinnamon and mix to combine. Pour the ganache into a piping bag or large sandwich bag. Cut a corner from the bag to create a small opening. Pipe the ganache into the molded shells, filling each shell three-quarters full. Gently tap the filled shells against the counter or table to release any trapped air bubbles. Let the ganache sit overnight at room temperature to dry.

4. To finish the molded chocolates: see page 109.

SALTED CARAMEL

This is, hands down, the best-selling piece of chocolate at Garrison Confections. While really quite a simple piece, nothing beats the smooth creaminess of the caramel, its full rich flavor, surrounded by deep, dark chocolate. And while the recipe does contain salt, you can't actually taste it. In fact, what the salt does is cut the sweetness of the caramel ever so slightly to perfectly balance out the overall flavor.

DIFFICULT   **Yield: 28 chocolates**

For chocolate shells:
2 pounds (906 g) 64 percent bittersweet chocolate, tempered

For salted caramel ganache:
4½ ounces (126 g) 29 percent white chocolate, chopped
1¼ ounces or 2½ tablespoons (35 g) granulated sugar
½ ounce or 1 tablespoon (14 g) water
3¼ ounce or 6½ tablespoons (91 g) heavy cream

¼ ounce or 1 teaspoon (7 g) light corn syrup
⅛ ounce or ½ teaspoon (4 g) Sel de Guerande
¾ ounce or 1½ tablespoons (21 g) salted butter, cubed, soft but not melted
¼ ounce (7 g) cocoa butter, melted, and cooled to body temperature

To finish chocolates:
8 ounces (224 g) 64 percent bittersweet chocolate, tempered

1. To prepare the molded shells: Mold the chocolate shells according to the procedure on page 108. Set aside until the chocolate has completely set and the shells are ready to be filled.

2. To make the ganache: Place the chopped chocolate in a medium-size bowl. Place the sugar and water in a medium-size, heavy-bottomed saucepan and stir together to form a wet sand. Place over high heat and cook until the sugar turns a dark amber color and begins to smoke. In the meantime, pour the cream, corn syrup, and salt into a small, heavy-bottomed saucepan, place over medium heat, and bring to a simmer. Carefully pour the hot cream mixture into the hot caramel. Do not pour too quickly or the mixture will boil over. When combined, immediately pour onto the chopped white chocolate. Let sit for 2 minutes to melt the chocolate. Stir slowly to incorporate. Using a candy thermometer placed in the center of the bowl, check the temperature. Once the ganache has reached 95°F (35°C), add the butter and cocoa butter, and mix to combine. Pour the ganache into a piping bag or large sandwich bag. Cut a corner from the bag to create a small opening. Pipe the ganache into the molded shells, filling each shell three-quarters full. Gently tap the filled shells against the counter or table to release any trapped air bubbles. Let the ganache sit overnight at room temperature to dry.

3. To finish the molded chocolates: see page 109.

Peanut Butter and Jam

Created by my inner child, these are a treat for any generation. Jam adds moisture to the overall texture, thereby slightly reducing the thickness of the peanut butter.

DIFFICULT   **Yield: 28 chocolates**

For chocolate shells:
2 pounds (906 g) 38 percent milk chocolate, tempered

For red raspberry jam layer:
3 ounces or ¼ cup (84 g) seedless red raspberry jam

For peanut butter ganache:
4½ ounces (126 g) 38 percent milk chocolate, chopped

4¼ ounces or scant ½ cup (119 g) creamy peanut butter
½ ounce (14 g) cocoa butter, melted and cooled to 95°F (35°C)
Pinch of salt

To finish chocolates:
8 ounces (224 g) 38 percent milk chocolate, tempered

---

1. To prepare the molded shells: Mold the chocolate shells according to the procedure on page 108. Set aside until the chocolate has completely set and shells are ready to be filled.

2. To make the raspberry jam layer: Place the raspberry jam in a bowl. Stir well to remove any lumps. Pour the jam into a piping bag or large sandwich bag. Cut a corner from the bag to create a small opening. Pipe the jam into the molded shells, filling each shell cavity half full. Gently tap the filled shells against the counter or table to release any trapped air bubbles. Set aside until ready to add the ganache.

3. To make the ganache: Place the milk chocolate in a medium-size microwaveable bowl. Heat in the microwave at 50 percent power for 20 seconds at a time, stirring between heatings, until fully melted. Using a candy thermometer placed in the center of the bowl, check the temperature. Once the chocolate has reached 95°F (35°C), combine with the peanut butter and stir well to incorporate. Add the cocoa butter and salt, and mix until combined. Pour the ganache into a piping bag or large sandwich bag. Cut a corner from the bag to create a small opening. Pipe the ganache into the molded shells on top of the jam layer, filling each shell cavity almost full. Gently tap the filled shells against the counter or table to release any trapped air bubbles. Let the ganache sit overnight at room temperature to dry.

4. To finish the molded chocolates: see page 109.

CANDY APPLE

I created this combination the first season I opened Garrison Confections, thinking it would be a signature piece in my chocolate collection that fall. To this day it is one of the chocolates customers still request. Meant to evoke memories of a harvest fair and apple-picking on a crisp autumn day, this piece is packed with flavors and myriad textures.

    If you cannot find apple essence, try a natural apple oil. Only use imitation as a last resort.

DIFFICULT   **Yield: 28 chocolates**

For chocolate shells:

2 pounds (906 g) 29 percent white chocolate, tempered

For white chocolate–caramel ganache:

4½ ounces (126 g) 29 percent white chocolate, chopped

1½ ounces or 3 tablespoons (42 g) granulated sugar

½ ounce or 1 tablespoon (14 g) water

3¼ ounces or 6½ tablespoons (91 g) heavy cream

¼ ounce or 1 teaspoon (7 g) light corn syrup

¼ ounce or 1½ teaspoons (7 g) salted butter, cubed, soft but not melted

4 drops Apple Essence or natural apple oil

To finish chocolates:

1 ounce (28 g) almonds, toasted, finely chopped

5 to 10 drops red food coloring

8 ounces (224 g) 29 percent white chocolate, tempered

1. To prepare the molded shells: Mold the chocolate shells according to the procedure on page 108. Set aside until the chocolate has completely set and the shells are ready to be filled.

2. To make the ganache: Place the chopped chocolate in a medium-size bowl. Place the sugar and water in a medium-size, heavy-bottomed saucepan and stir together to form a wet sand. Place over high heat and cook until the sugar turns a dark amber color and begins to smoke. In the meantime, pour the cream and corn syrup into a small, heavy-bottomed saucepan, place over medium heat, and bring to a simmer. Carefully pour the hot cream mixture into the hot caramel. Do not pour too quickly or the mixture

will boil over. When combined, immediately pour onto the chopped chocolate. Let sit for 2 minutes to melt the chocolate. Stir slowly to incorporate. Using a candy thermometer placed in the center of the bowl, check the temperature. Once the ganache has reached 95°F (35°C), add the butter and apple essence, and mix to combine. Pour the ganache into a piping bag or large sandwich bag. Cut a corner from the bag to create a small opening. Pipe the ganache into the molded shells, filling each shell three-quarters full. Gently tap the filled shells against the counter or table to release any trapped air bubbles. Let the ganache sit overnight at room temperature to dry.

3. To finish the molded chocolates: Mix the toasted almonds with 5 to 10 drops of red food coloring. Set aside. Ladle approximately 4 to 8 ounces (112 to 224 g) of tempered chocolate onto the top of the filled shells. Using a large offset spatula, spread the chocolate evenly across the top of the mold, making sure to completely cover the entire surface. Scrape off any excess chocolate into the bowl. Sprinkle the almonds over the top of the shells, enough to cover the white chocolate completely. Gently push down on the almonds to help them adhere to the white chocolate, but be careful not to press too hard. Put the mold in the refrigerator for 10 to 15 minutes, or until the chocolate has released from the sides of the mold. Remove from the refrigerator and allow the chocolates to come to room temperature before unmolding. Invert the mold over a sheet of parchment paper, and gently tap the mold against the counter to release the chocolates.

TRIPLE ESPRESSO–VANILLA

This chocolate is different than any of the others in this chapter as it is truly a two-layer piece, composed of a vanilla ganache on top of a coffee ganache. When you bite into this chocolate, you will notice its two distinct colors.

I chose to mold this piece in dark chocolate as I feel the flavor strength of that chocolate is not overshadowed by the strong coffee flavor and yet still provides a nice contrast to the vanilla ganache.

Just as you should use the best vanilla beans you can, try to find the best-flavored coffee beans possible and grind them yourself just before making this recipe, for optimal freshness.

DIFFICULT   **Yield: 28 chocolates**

For chocolate shells:
2 pounds (906 g) 64 percent bittersweet chocolate, tempered

For vanilla ganache:
6¼ ounces (175 g) 29 percent white chocolate, chopped
2¾ ounces or ⅓ cup (77 g) heavy cream
1 vanilla bean, split and scraped
¾ ounce or 1½ tablespoons (21 g) salted butter, cubed, soft but not melted

For coffee paste:
¼ ounce or full 1 tablespoon (7 g) freshly ground coffee, preferably Italian
3 ounces or 6 tablespoons (84 g) water

For triple espresso ganache:
1¾ ounces (49 g) 38 percent milk chocolate, chopped
½ ounce (14 g) 55 percent semisweet chocolate, chopped
1 ounce or 3 tablespoons (28 g) whole milk
¼ ounce or full 1 tablespoon (7 g) freshly ground coffee, preferably Italian
¼ ounce or 1 teaspoon (7 g) light corn syrup
½ ounce or 2 teaspoons (14 g) coffee paste

To finish chocolates:
8 ounces (224 g) 64 percent bittersweet chocolate, tempered

1. To prepare the molded shells: Mold the chocolate shells according to the procedure on page 108. Set aside until the chocolate has completely set and the shells are ready to be filled.

2. To make the vanilla ganache: Place the chopped chocolate in a medium-size bowl. Pour the cream into a small, heavy-bottomed saucepan and add the vanilla bean seeds. Cook the cream mixture over medium-high heat until it begins to simmer. Remove from heat, cover the saucepan, and let the cream and beans steep for 15 minutes. Return the saucepan to the stove, uncovered, and cook over medium-high heat until the cream mixture reaches a rolling boil. Immediately pour through a fine-mesh sieve onto the chopped chocolate. Let the ganache sit for 2 minutes to melt the chocolate. Stir slowly to incorporate. Using a candy thermometer placed in the center of the bowl, check the temperature. Once the ganache has reached 95°F (35°C), add the butter and mix to combine. Pour the ganache into a piping bag or large sandwich bag. Cut a corner from the bag to create a small opening. Pipe the ganache into the molded shells, filling each shell half-full. Gently tap the filled shells against the counter or table to release any trapped air bubbles. Place mold in the refrigerator for 10 minutes or until vanilla layer is set. Then, begin preparing the triple espresso layer.

3. To make the coffee paste: Place the ground coffee in a small bowl. Bring the water to a rapid boil, pour over the coffee, and stir to dissolve the coffee grounds. Set aside until ready to use. This will make more than the required amount. The remaining paste can be stored in the refrigerator in an airtight container, but must be stirred thoroughly before each use.

4. To make the triple espresso ganache: Place the chopped chocolate in a medium-size bowl. Pour the milk into a small, heavy-bottomed saucepan and add the coffee. Cook over medium-high heat until the mixture begins to simmer.

Remove from heat, and let it steep for 2 minutes. Strain through a fine-mesh sieve into a clean bowl or measuring cup. Measure or weigh out $3/4$ ounce or 2 tablespoons (21 g) and place into a clean, small, heavy-bottomed saucepan.(If the mixture falls short of the required amount, add enough heavy cream to make up the amount.) Add the corn syrup and cook over medium-high heat to a rapid boil. Pour onto the chopped chocolate. Let sit for 2 minutes to melt the chocolate. Stir slowly to incorporate. Using a candy thermometer placed in the center of the bowl, check the temperature. Once the ganache has reached 95°F (35°C), add the coffee paste and stir to combine. Pour the ganache into a piping bag or large sandwich bag. Cut a corner from the bag to create a small opening. Pipe the ganache into the molded shells over the vanilla ganache layer, filling each shell almost full. Gently tap the filled shells against the counter or table to release any trapped air bubbles. Let the ganache sit overnight at room temperature to dry.

5. To finish the molded chocolates: see page 109.

Chapter Seven

Hand–Dipped
Chocolates

Hand-dipped chocolates are a cross between a truffle and a molded chocolate. Like truffles, the fillings are made first and then the shells are applied. Hand-dipped pieces are generally square or rectangular, like many molded ones, and are able to accommodate a wide variety of fillings.

Traditionally, hand-dipped chocolates were plain brown on the outside and often decorated with textures or pieces of candied fruit or nuts. This would also be a clue as to what the inside might be. Modern hand-dipped chocolates are bright with colored patterns and logos, which are adhered to the chocolates via the use of transfer sheets and colored cocoa butter. Chocolatiers have realized that consumers first eat with their eyes, and more emphasis is being placed on creating chocolates that look as fabulous as they taste.

This chapter will build upon the techniques learned making truffles and molded chocolates while broadening your chocolate-making skills. Once you have mastered how to hand-dip chocolates and understand the types of fillings that work well with this application, try your hand at adding fun designs and textures to make these chocolate creations your own.

Right: Raspberry-Wasabi, page 144

While a 10 or 20 percent difference in the amount of light cream used to make a ganache may not seem significant, it is these small nuances that differentiate good chocolates from great ones.

What You Will Need to Get Started

Because the centers are created first and then dipped in chocolate, molds are not necessary. You can use either custom-made stainless-steel frames or a heavy-duty baking pan to pour your centers. You will want to make sure to use a pan that will easily release the centers once they have set. The recipes in this chapter were tested using an 8" (20.3 cm) square nonstick cake pan.

To Prepare the Pan

To make the recipes in this chapter, spray an 8" (20.3 cm) square pan with nonstick cooking spray. Line the sides and bottom of the pan with plastic wrap, smoothing to remove any wrinkles.

Fillings and Flavors

Hand-dipped chocolates have an advantage over truffles and molded chocolates because there are more filling options. In addition to working well with ganaches, nut pastes, and jams as centers, *pâtes de fruit* (fruit jellies) may also be added. Because hand-dipped centers are made in layers, fruit jellies can be poured over ganache or nut pastes, and allowed to set before being covered in chocolate.

Ganache used in hand-dipped chocolates is slightly different than that used in truffles or molded pieces. Truffle ganache contains 20 percent less heavy cream, and molded ganache, 10 percent more. This means that using truffle ganache would yield a drier, heavier piece whereas molded ganache would be loose and not set well, making the centers challenging to dip.

Hand-dipped chocolates brushed with luster dust

Hand-Dipped Chocolates

The general procedure for making hand-dipped centers is as follows: Make the ganache, nut paste, or *pâte de fruit* as specified in the recipe. Pour it into a frame or baking pan and allow to set. If making a double-layer center, repeat as necessary. Once the center has cooled and set, remove it from the baking pan or frame and place on a clean work surface. Apply the foot then release onto parchment paper. Use a ruler or unflavored dental floss to mark how and where you want to cut the chocolates. Use a large, sharp chef's knife to cut each individual piece. Separate the pieces from each other to allow air to dry all their sides.

1. Pour the filling into the pan and allow to set firmly.

2. Add a second layer if called for in the recipe.

3. Gently flip onto a clean, dry cutting board and remove the plastic from the bottom of the set center.

4. To create a foot, spread a thin layer of melted chocolate over the set ganache.

5. Cut the center into individual pieces.

How to Hand-Dip Centers

Once the centers are made, allow to set overnight, and then cut. They are now ready to be dipped. You will need a large bowl of tempered chocolate for this, as well as a parchment paper-lined baking sheet. Dip the centers one by one to avoid making a mess. Place each center onto the middle of a dipping fork or large dinner fork, and completely submerge the fork and its center into the tempered chocolate before pulling it back out. You may need to repeat this step a couple of times to fully coat the center in chocolate. Gently tap the handle of the fork and scrape the bottom of the fork against the side of the bowl to help remove any excess chocolate. Transfer the dipped piece onto the clean sheet of parchment paper to set.

1. Dip the center in tempered chocolate.

2. Scrape bottom of fork against side of bowl to remove excess chocolate.

3. Angling the fork, transfer the dipped piece to paper to set.

How to Modernize Hand-Dipped Chocolates

Once you have mastered dipping the centers, it is easy to add either a colored or textured design to the top of each piece. Colored designs are added by using transfer sheets made with colored cocoa butter. The idea is pretty simple. Remember when you were a kid and wanted to put a temporary tattoo on your hand? You would wet the area, put the tattoo on face down, rub it, and let it set for a couple of minutes before peeling back the paper. Lo and behold, the tattoo would have transferred from the paper onto your hand. Transferring designs onto chocolate follows the same basic principle. Some transfer sheets apply a textured pattern to a chocolate rather than a colored design.

Professional chocolatiers often have their own transfer sheets created or use stock patterns available to the industry. However, you can make your own colored transfer sheets at home with materials easily found at candy-making, arts-and-crafts, and floral-supply stores. Just remember to use only culinary-grade materials when making your own sheets, and to use clean tools and brushes reserved exclusively for your chocolate making.

To make a colored design transfer sheet, start with a piece of food-safe acetate or Mylar. Heat the colored cocoa butter enough to melt and make it fluid. Cool down the melted cocoa butter to 93.2°F to 96.8°F (34°C to 36°C). Spread the cocoa butter onto the acetate using a woodgrain tool, a toothbrush, a fingernail brush, your finger, a paintbrush, or whatever other tool you want to create the desired pattern. If using various colors, allow each to cool and set completely before adding another, or the colors will smudge and smear together. Allow the design to set completely before cutting to size and applying it to the chocolate.

TIP:

Textures may also be applied by hand, by dragging a dipping fork across the top of the freshly dipped chocolate.

1. Add colored cocoa butter to acetate or Mylar.

2. Create the pattern.

3. When the pattern is set, cut into strips.

4. Cut the strips into squares slightly larger than the size of the cut centers.

5. Gently press transfer sheet face down onto the top of the freshly dipped chocolate and rub the top of sheet with fork.

6. Wait until the chocolate sets and the sheet looks like it is starting to release before gently peeling back the transfer sheet to release the design.

BITTERSWEET 64 PERCENT

Using a 64 percent dark chocolate for this piece will result in a nice overall chocolate flavor without being too strong.

EASY   **Yield: 42 chocolates**

For ganache:
10 ounces (280 g) 64 percent bittersweet chocolate, chopped
8 ounces or 1 cup (224 g) heavy cream
1 ounce or 1 tablespoon plus 1 teaspoon (28 g) light corn syrup
1 ounce or 2 tablespoons (28 g) salted butter, cubed, soft but not melted

For the foot:
5¼ ounces (147 g) 64 percent bittersweet chocolate, melted

To dip and decorate the chocolates:
2 pounds (906 g) 64 percent bittersweet chocolate, tempered

1. To make the ganache: Place the chocolate in a medium-size bowl and set aside. Combine the heavy cream and corn syrup in a small, heavy-bottomed saucepan and cook over medium-high heat. Stir until the mixture comes to a full boil. Immediately pour onto the chopped chocolate. Let sit for 2 minutes and then stir to combine. Using a candy thermometer placed in the center of the bowl, check the temperature. Once the ganache has reached 95°F (35°C), stir in the butter. Immediately pour the ganache into the prepared pan (see page 128). Spread evenly using a small offset spatula, knocking the pan if necessary to release any trapped air bubbles. Place the ganache in the freezer for 30 minutes. Once the ganache is firm, remove from the freezer.

2. To add the foot: Remove the ganache from the pan by picking up both sides of the plastic wrap. Gently flip the ganache over onto a baking sheet covered with a clean piece of plastic wrap or sheet of parchment paper, so the ganache is now bottom side up. Peel the plastic off the bottom of the ganache. Heat the foot chocolate in the microwave on 50 percent power for 20 seconds at a time, until it is completely melted. To create a foot, spread a thin layer of the melted chocolate over the chocolate ganache, using a small offset spatula. Place in the freezer for 2 hours to set.

3. To cut the filling: Remove the ganache from the freezer and gently flip onto a parchment paper-lined cutting board so the foot is face down. Using a sharp, nonserrated knife, trim all four edges. Use a ruler to mark the ganache on all four sides at 1" (2.5 cm) intervals. Match up the notches and cut the pieces into squares. Separate the squares onto parchment paper. Allow the squares to sit overnight at room temperature to dry.

4. To dip and decorate the chocolates: To dip, see page 131. Decorate as desired.

Grand Marnier

Grand Marnier is a classic flavor found in chocolate. This is one of my favorite combinations.

EASY   **Yield: 42 chocolates**

For ganache:
3 3/4 ounces (105 g) 64 percent bittersweet chocolate, chopped
6 ounces (168 g) 55 percent semisweet chocolate, chopped
7 1/2 ounces or 1 cup minus 1 tablespoon (210 g) heavy cream
1/2 ounce or 2 teaspoons (14 g) light corn syrup
3/4 ounce or 1 1/2 tablespoons (21 g) salted butter, cubed, soft but not melted

1 ounce or 1/4 cup (28 g) Grand Marnier
1 drop natural orange oil

For the foot:
5 1/4 ounces (147 g) 64 percent bittersweet chocolate, melted

To dip and decorate the chocolates:
2 pounds (906 g) 64 percent bittersweet chocolate, tempered
42 pieces candied orange peel, sliced

---

1. To make the ganache: Place the chocolate in a medium-size bowl and set aside. Combine the heavy cream and corn syrup in a small, heavy-bottomed saucepan and cook over medium-high heat. Stir until the cream mixture comes to a full boil. Immediately pour onto the chopped chocolate. Let sit for 2 minutes and then stir to combine. Using a candy thermometer placed in the center of the bowl, check the temperature. Once the ganache has reached 95°F (35°C), stir in the butter, Grand Marnier, and orange oil. Immediately pour the ganache into the prepared pan (see page 128). Spread evenly using a small offset spatula, knocking the pan if necessary to release any trapped air bubbles. Place the ganache in the freezer for 30 minutes. Once the ganache is firm, remove from the freezer.

2. To add the foot: Remove the ganache from the pan by picking up both sides of the plastic wrap. Gently flip the ganache over onto a baking sheet covered with a clean piece of plastic wrap or sheet of parchment paper so the ganache is

now bottom side up. Peel the plastic off the bottom of the ganache. Heat the foot chocolate in the microwave on 50 percent power for 20 seconds at a time, until it is completely melted. To create a foot, spread a thin layer of the melted chocolate over the chocolate ganache, using a small offset spatula. Place in the freezer for 2 hours to set.

3. To cut the filling: Remove the ganache from the freezer and gently flip onto a parchment paper-lined cutting board so the foot is face down. Using a sharp, nonserrated knife, trim all four edges. Use a ruler to mark the ganache on all four sides at 1" (2.5 cm) intervals. Match up the notches and cut the pieces into squares. Separate the squares onto parchment paper. Allow the squares to sit overnight at room temperature to dry.

4. To dip and decorate the chocolates: To dip, see page 131. To decorate place a candied orange slice on top of each chocolate while wet.

JASMINE TEA

Tea is generally a great flavor combination with chocolate. Even if you are not a tea drinker, you will appreciate how the tea's subtle flavor blends seamlessly into a ganache and stands up to the chocolate.

I have chosen to apply two decorations to this piece: half of each square is sprinkled with fresh tea while the other half is decorated with a textured transfer sheet. This type of decor is a good example of how you can mix and match different techniques to create your own unique look.

EASY   **Yield: 42 chocolates**

For ganache:
9³⁄4 ounces (273 g) 64 percent bittersweet chocolate, chopped
5 ounces or scant ²⁄3 cup (140 g) heavy cream
2 ounces or ¼ cup (56 g) water
½ ounce or ¼ cup (14 g) loose jasmine tea
½ ounce or 2 teaspoons (14 g) light corn syrup
2 ounces or ¼ cup (56 g) salted butter, cubed, soft but not melted

For the foot:
5¼ ounces (147 g) 38 percent milk chocolate, melted

To dip and decorate the chocolates:
2 pounds (906 g) 38 percent milk chocolate, tempered
⅛ ounce or 3 teaspoons (3.5 g) loose jasmine tea

---

1. To make the ganache: Place the chocolate in a medium-size bowl and set aside. Combine the heavy cream, water, and tea in a small, heavy-bottomed saucepan and cook over medium-high heat. Stir until the mixture comes to a simmer. Remove from heat and cover. Allow the mixture to steep for 10 minutes. Strain through a fine-mesh sieve into a clean bowl or measuring cup. Weigh or measure out 5 ounces or ²⁄3 cup (145 g) and pour into a clean, small, heavy-bottomed saucepan. (If the mixture does not yield required amount, make up the difference with fresh heavy cream.) Add the corn syrup and cook over medium-high heat until the mixture comes to a rapid boil. Immediately pour over chopped chocolate. Let sit for 2 minutes and then stir to combine. Using a candy thermometer placed in the center of the bowl, check the temperature. Once the ganache has reached 95°F

(35°C), stir in the butter. Immediately pour the ganache into the prepared pan (see page 128). Spread evenly using a small offset spatula, knocking the pan if necessary to release any trapped air bubbles. Place the ganache in the freezer for 30 minutes. Once the ganache is firm, remove from the freezer.

2. To add the foot: Remove the ganache from the pan by picking up both sides of the plastic wrap. Gently flip the ganache over onto a baking sheet covered with a clean piece of plastic wrap or sheet of parchment paper so the ganache is now bottom side up. Peel the plastic off the bottom of the ganache. Heat the foot chocolate in the microwave on 50 percent power for 20 seconds at a time, until it is completely melted. To create a foot, spread a thin layer of the melted chocolate over the chocolate ganache, using a small offset spatula. Place in the freezer for 2 hours to set.

3. To cut the filling: Remove the ganache from the freezer and gently flip onto a parchment paper-lined cutting board so the foot is face down. Using a sharp, nonserrated knife, trim all four edges. Use a ruler to mark the ganache on all four sides at 1" (2.5 cm) intervals. Match up the notches and cut the pieces into squares. Separate the squares onto parchment paper.

Allow the squares to sit overnight at room temperature to dry.

4. To dip and decorate the chocolates: To dip, see page 101. To decorate, lightly sprinkle fresh loose tea diagonally across half of the dipped square. Next, gently press a prepared transfer piece down diagonally on top of the other side of the dipped square. Smooth out the top of the chocolate by lightly running the dipping fork over the transfer sheet. Repeat the dipping and decorating process with the remaining squares.

COFFEE-HAZELNUT

While hazelnut is a classic chocolate center, the addition of coffee modernizes this combination. I also happen to think that the flavor profiles of the coffee and hazelnuts stand up to each other nicely.

This piece is an example of a two-textured dipped center: a creamy ganache over a praline layer. When you bite into the chocolate you get a nice crunch to complement the smoothness. You could also omit the coffee flavor in the ganache for a hazelnut–dark chocolate combination.

MEDIUM   **Yield: 42 chocolates**

For hazelnut praline:

3½ ounces (98 g) whole hazelnuts, skin on, toasted

7 ounces or ¾ cup plus 2 tablespoons (196 g) granulated sugar

¾ ounce or 1½ tablespoons (21 g) water

For milk chocolate praline:

3¼ ounces (91 g) 38 percent milk chocolate, melted and cooled to 90°F (32°C)

7 ounces or ¾ cup (196 g) hazelnut praline, room temperature

¼ ounce (7 g) cocoa butter, melted and cooled to 90°F (32°C)

For coffee ganache:

4¼ ounces (119 g) 64 percent bittersweet chocolate, chopped

3½ ounces or ½ cup minus 1 tablespoon (98 g) heavy cream

¾ ounce or ¼ cup (21 g) freshly ground coffee, preferably Italian

¼ ounce or 1 teaspoon (7 g) light corn syrup

¾ ounce or 1½ tablespoons (21 g) salted butter, cubed, soft but not melted

½ ounce or 2 tablespoons (14 g) coffee-flavored liqueur

For the foot:

5¼ ounces (147 g) 38 percent milk chocolate, melted

To dip and decorate the chocolates:

2 pounds (906 g) 38 percent milk chocolate, tempered

42 whole hazelnuts, skin removed, toasted

1. To make the hazelnut praline: Place the toasted hazelnuts on a baking sheet lined with a Silpat and set aside. Combine the sugar and water in a small, heavy-bottomed saucepan and cook over high heat. Do not stir the sugar. If the edges start to burn, swirl the pot around a few times to coat the sides of the pan with water, and place the pan back on the heat. Cook the sugar to a smoking dark amber caramel. Remove from heat and carefully pour directly over the hazelnuts. Let cool completely. Break the caramelized hazelnut slab into pieces and put in a food processor. Grind to a pasty liquid consistency, making sure no large hazelnut chunks remain. This should take 5 to 10 minutes in the food processor. Store the hazelnut praline in the refrigerator in an airtight container until ready to use. Hazelnut praline can also be stored in the freezer for a longer period of time. Thaw in the refrigerator overnight prior to using.

2. To make the milk chocolate praline layer: Combine the chocolate and the hazelnut praline. Add the cocoa butter and stir until ingredients are incorporated. Pour into the prepared pan (see page 128). Spread evenly using a small offset spatula, knocking the pan if necessary to release any trapped air bubbles. Place the praline in the refrigerator for 30 minutes. Once the layer is firm, remove from the refrigerator and begin the next layer.

3. To make the ganache: Place the chocolate in a medium-size bowl and set aside. Combine heavy cream and ground coffee in a small, heavy-bottomed saucepan and cook over medium-high heat. Stir until the mixture comes to a simmer. Remove from heat and cover for 10 minutes. After the coffee has steeped in the cream, strain the cream through a fine-mesh sieve into a clean bowl or measuring cup, and weigh out or measure 3½ ounces or ½ cup (102 g) of the cream mixture. (If necessary, add fresh cream to reach required amount.) Pour into a clean, small, heavy-bottomed saucepan, add the corn syrup and place over medium-high heat. Bring to a rapid boil, remove from heat, and pour over the chopped chocolate. Let sit for 2 minutes and then stir to combine. Using a candy thermometer placed in the center of the bowl, check the temperature. Once the ganache has reached 95°F (35°C), stir in the butter and coffee-flavored liqueur. Pour the ganache into the pan over the praline layer. Spread evenly using a small offset spatula, knocking the pan if necessary to release any trapped air bubbles. Place the ganache in the freezer for 30 minutes. Once the ganache is firm, remove from the freezer.

4. To add the foot: Remove the ganache from the pan by picking up both sides of the plastic wrap. Gently flip the ganache over onto a baking sheet covered with a clean piece of plastic wrap or sheet of parchment paper so the praline layer is now bottom side up. Peel the plastic off the bottom of the praline. Heat the foot chocolate in the microwave on 50 percent power for 20 seconds at a time, until it is completely melted. To create a foot, spread a thin layer of the melted chocolate over the chocolate ganache, using a small offset spatula. Place in the freezer for 2 hours to set.

5. To cut the filling: Remove the layers from the freezer and gently flip onto a parchment paper-lined cutting board so the foot is face down. Using a sharp, nonserrated knife, trim all four edges. Use a ruler to mark the ganache on all four sides at 1" (2.5 cm) intervals. Match up the notches and cut into squares. Separate the squares onto parchment paper. Allow the squares to sit overnight at room temperature to dry.

6. To dip and decorate the chocolates: To dip, see page 131. To decorate, tap the end of a 908 Ateco pastry tip in the middle of the top of the dipped square, then place a toasted hazelnut in the center of the design. Repeat the dipping and decorating process with the remaining squares.

GINGER CRUNCH

Ginger is substituted for the salt to create a variation on the salted caramel chocolate in chapter six.

MEDIUM   **Yield: 42 chocolates**

For caramel crunch:
1¾ ounces or scant ¼ cup (49 g) granulated sugar
¾ ounce or 1 tablespoon (21 g) light corn syrup

For ginger-caramel ganache:
4 ounces (112 g) 72 percent extra-bittersweet chocolate, chopped
4 ounces (112 g) 29 percent white chocolate, chopped
2½ ounces or ⅓ cup (70 g) granulated sugar
1 ounce or 2 tablespoons (28 g) water
5¾ ounces or ⅔ cup (161 g) heavy cream
¼ ounce or 1 teaspoon (7 g) light corn syrup

¼ ounce (7 g) cocoa butter, melted and cooled to 90°F (32°C)
¾ ounce or 1½ tablespoons (21 g) salted butter, cubed, soft but not melted
Pinch ground ginger

For the foot:
5¼ ounces (147 g) 38 percent milk chocolate, melted

To dip and decorate chocolates:
2 pounds (906 g) 38 percent milk chocolate, tempered
42 candied ginger slices

---

1. To make the caramel crunch: Place one Silpat right side up on a heat-resistant countertop or table. Combine the granulated sugar and corn syrup in a small, heavy-bottomed saucepan and place over medium-high heat. Do not stir. Cook the sugar until it reaches a medium amber color. Immediately and carefully pour the hot sugar mixture onto the Silpat. Place a second Silpat on top of the first, and gently and carefully roll flat using a rolling pin. Set aside for 10 to 20 minutes to cool. Peel off the top Silpat, break up the caramel into shards, and place in a food processor. Pulse the shards into a coarse powder. Set aside until ready to use.

2. To make the ganache: Place the chocolate in a medium-size bowl and set aside. Place the

sugar and water in a medium-size, heavy-bottomed saucepan and stir together to form a wet sand. Place over high heat and cook until the sugar turns a dark amber color and begins to smoke. In the meantime, pour the cream and corn syrup into a small, heavy-bottomed saucepan, place over medium heat and bring to a simmer. Carefully pour the hot cream into the hot caramel. Do not pour too quickly or the mixture will boil over. When combined, immediately pour onto the chopped chocolate. Let sit for 2 minutes and then stir to combine. Using a candy thermometer placed in the center of the bowl, check the temperature. Once the ganache has reached 95°F (35°C), stir in the cocoa butter, butter, and ginger. Fold in the crunch and stir until fully incorporated. Pour the ganache into the prepared pan (see page 128). Spread evenly using a small offset spatula, knocking the pan if necessary to release any trapped air bubbles. Place the ganache in the freezer for 2 hours. Once the ganache is firm, remove from the freezer.

3. To add the foot: Remove the ganache from the pan by picking up both sides of the plastic wrap. Gently flip the ganache over onto a baking sheet covered with a clean piece of plastic wrap or sheet of parchment paper so the ganache is now bottom side up. Peel the plastic off the bottom of the ganache. Heat the foot chocolate in the microwave on 50 percent power for 20 seconds at a time, until it is completely melted. To create a foot, spread a thin layer of the melted chocolate over the chocolate ganache, using a small offset spatula. Place in the freezer for 2 hours to set.

4. To cut the filling: Remove the ganache from the freezer and gently flip onto parchment paper-lined cutting board so the foot is face down. Using a sharp, nonserrated knife, trim all four edges. Use a ruler to mark the ganache on all four sides at 1" (2.5 cm) intervals. Match up the notches and cut into squares. Separate the squares onto parchment paper. Allow the squares to sit overnight at room temperature to dry.

5. To dip and decorate the chocolates: To dip, see page 131. To decorate, place a candied ginger slice on top of each piece while the chocolate is still wet. Repeat the dipping and decorating process with the remaining squares.

FIVE-SPICE PRALINE

Chinese five-spice powder is a blend of different spices that could be a combination of any of the following: fennel, cloves, cinnamon, star anise, Szechuan peppercorn, ginger, nutmeg, or licorice, depending on the blending house. A staple in the Chinese pantry, this powder is reputed to enliven even the blandest dish as it encompasses all five flavors: bitter, salty, sweet, pungent, and sour.

MEDIUM **Yield: 42 chocolates**

For hazelnut praline:

4 ounces (112 g) whole hazelnuts, skin on, toasted

4 ounces (112 g) whole hazelnuts, skin removed, toasted

5½ ounces or full ¾ cup (154 g) granulated sugar

¾ ounce or 1½ tablespoons (21 g) water

For five-spice ganache:

13½ ounces or 2⅓ cups (385 g) hazelnut praline

3½ ounces (98 g) 38 percent milk chocolate, melted and cooled to 90°F (32°C)

1½ ounces (42 g) cocoa butter, melted and cooled to 90°F (32°C)

1¼ ounces or ½ cup (35 g) feuillantines (thin crêpe cookies, crushed)

Pinch Chinese five-spice powder

For the foot:

5¼ ounces (147 g) 38 percent milk chocolate, melted

To dip and decorate chocolates:

2 pounds (906 g) 38 percent milk chocolate, tempered

Shredded coconut, toasted, to taste

1. To make the praline: Place the toasted hazelnuts on a baking sheet lined with a Silpat and set aside. Combine the sugar and water in a small, heavy-bottomed saucepan and cook over high heat. Do not stir the sugar. If the edges start to burn, swirl the pot around a few times to coat the sides of the pan with water, and place the pan back on the heat. Cook the sugar to a smoking dark amber caramel. Remove from heat and carefully pour directly over the hazelnuts. Let cool completely. Break the caramelized hazelnut slab into pieces and put in food processor. Grind to a pasty liquid consistency, making sure no large hazelnut chunks remain. This should take 5 to 10 minutes in the food processor.

Store the hazelnut praline in the refrigerator in an airtight container until ready to use. Hazelnut praline can also be stored in the freezer for a longer period of time. Thaw in the refrigerator overnight prior to using.

2. To make the ganache: Combine the hazelnut praline and the milk chocolate. Add the cocoa butter and mix. Gently fold in the feuillantines and five-spice powder. Pour the ganache directly into the prepared pan (see page 128). Spread evenly using a small offset spatula, knocking the pan if necessary to release any trapped air bubbles. Place the ganache in the freezer for 30 minutes. Once the ganache is firm, remove from the freezer.

3. To add the foot: Remove the ganache from the pan by picking up both sides of the plastic wrap. Gently flip the ganache over onto a baking sheet covered with a clean piece of plastic wrap or sheet of parchment paper so the ganache is now bottom side up. Peel the plastic off the bottom of the ganache. Heat the foot chocolate in the microwave on 50 percent power for 20 seconds at a time, until it is completely melted. To create a foot, spread a thin layer of the melted chocolate over the chocolate ganache, using a small offset spatula. Place in the freezer for 2 hours to set.

4. To cut the filling: Remove the ganache from the freezer and gently flip onto parchment paper-lined cutting board so the foot is face down.

Using a sharp, nonserrated knife, trim all four edges. Use a ruler to mark the ganache on all four sides at 1" (2.5 cm) intervals. Match up the notches and cut the pieces into squares. Separate the squares onto parchment paper. Allow the squares to sit overnight at room temperature to dry.

5. To dip and decorate the chocolates: To dip, see page 131. To decorate, sprinkle a pinch of toasted coconut on top of each dipped piece while the chocolate is still wet. Repeat the dipping and decorating process with the remaining squares.

RASPBERRY–WASABI

This flavor combination is one of my new favorites. When I first made it, I was pleasantly surprised by the way the flavors complemented each other. The slight sting of the wasabi is nicely balanced by the sweetness and acidity of the raspberry.

This recipe is slightly more difficult to make than previous recipes, as it uses a *pâte de fruit,* or a fruit jelly layer. The results, however, are well worth the extra effort. Use *g pectin*, a custom-formulated pectin that I developed. Regular pectin from the grocery store will not produce the desired consistency needed for the *pâte de fruit* to hold its shape.

If you like the combination of raspberry with milk chocolate, you can also omit the wasabi from the recipe. Likewise, you can substitute fresh lemon zest for wasabi; just remember to strain the cream before making the ganache.

DIFFICULT　**Yield: 42 chocolates**

For raspberry purée:
1 pound (453 g) fresh or frozen raspberries, thawed
1½ ounces or 7 tablespoons (42 g) confectioners' sugar

For raspberry *pâte de fruit*:
5 ounces or ½ cup (140 g) raspberry purée
4¼ ounces or full ½ cup (119 g) granulated sugar
½ ounce or 2 tablespoons (14 g) g pectin

For raspberry ganache:
5¼ ounces (147 g) 38 percent milk chocolate, chopped
¾ ounce (21 g) 61 percent dark chocolate, chopped

2 ounces or ¼ cup (56 g) heavy cream
¼ ounce or 1 teaspoon (7 g) light corn syrup
1 ounce or 2½ tablespoons (28 g) raspberry purée
¼ ounce or 1½ teaspoons (7 g) salted butter, cubed, soft but not melted
¼ ounce or full 1 tablespoon (7 g) raspberry liqueur
Pinch wasabi powder

For the foot:
5¼ ounces (147 g) 61 percent bittersweet dark chocolate, melted

To dip and decorate chocolates:
2 pounds (906 g) 61 percent dark chocolate, tempered

---

1. To make the raspberry purée: Combine the raspberries and sugar in a food processor. Process the fruit on a low speed until completely liquid. Strain through a fine mesh sieve into a clean bowl. Cover with plastic wrap and keep refrigerated until ready to use.

2. To make the raspberry *pâte de fruit*: Place the purée and half of the sugar in a small, heavy-bottomed saucepan. In a separate bowl, whisk together the other half of the sugar with the g pectin. Heat the purée mixture over medium heat while whisking vigorously. Once the mixture comes to a boil, whisk in the g pectin mixture. Continue to whisk, allowing mixture to come to a second boil. Whisk for 2 minutes more and remove from heat. Pour directly into the prepared pan (see page 128). Shake the pan to spread the *pâte de fruit* into all the crevices. Chill for 20 minutes in the refrigerator. After 20 minutes, let the pan sit at room temperature.

3. To make the ganache: Combine the chopped chocolates in a medium-size bowl and set aside. Combine the heavy cream, corn syrup, and raspberry purée in a small, heavy-bottomed saucepan and cook over medium-high heat. Stir until the mixture comes to a full boil. Immediately pour onto the chocolate. Stir to combine. Using a candy thermometer placed in the center of the bowl, check the temperature. Once the ganache has reached 95°F (35°C), stir in the butter, rasp-

berry liquor, and wasabi powder. Immediately pour directly over the raspberry *pâte de fruit* layer. Spread evenly using a small offset spatula, knocking the pan if necessary to release any trapped air bubbles. Place the ganache in the freezer for 1 hour. Once the ganache is firm, remove from the freezer.

4. To add the foot: Remove the ganache from the pan by picking up both sides of the plastic wrap. Gently transfer the ganache onto a baking sheet covered with a clean sheet of parchment paper so the ganache is still on top. Heat the foot chocolate in the microwave on 50 percent power for 20 seconds at a time, until it is completely melted. To create a foot, spread a thin layer of the melted chocolate over the chocolate ganache, using a small offset spatula. Place in the freezer for 1 hour.

5. To cut the filling: Remove the layers from the freezer and gently flip onto a parchment paper-lined cutting board so the foot is face down and the fruit layer is on top. Gently peel off the plastic wrap. Using a sharp, nonserrated knife, trim all four edges. Use a ruler to mark the ganache on all four sides at 1" (2.5 cm) intervals. Match up the notches and cut the pieces into squares. Separate the squares onto parchment paper. Allow the squares to sit overnight at room temperature to dry.

6. To dip and decorate the chocolates: To dip, see page 131. Decorate as desired or sprinkle with fresh wasabi powder.

STRAWBERRY–BALSAMIC

My first job as a pastry chef was at the Locanda dell'Amorosa, a gracious restaurant and hotel in the Tuscany region of Italy. The property had its own orchards and farm lands, and every day I would pick fresh fruit to use in my desserts. When in season, the strawberries were succulent and flavorful, sweet with juice, a natural pairing with Italy's prized vinegar, aged balsamic vinegar from Modena.

The key to this recipe is to use the freshest strawberries you can in season and combine them with the best balsamic vinegar you can afford. The sweetness of the strawberries counteracts the tang of the vinegar and enhances the balsamic flavor.

When you eat one of these chocolates you will predominantly taste the strawberry. The balsamic vinegar flavor will come next and linger after your last swallow. It's quite interesting, actually.

If you like the combination of strawberries and balsamic vinegar, try it as an ice-cream topping or even as dessert. Chop up some fresh strawberries, liberally sprinkle them with granulated sugar, and then add balsamic vinegar to taste. Delicious on a summer day!

DIFFICULT   **Yield: 42 chocolates**

For strawberry purée:
1 pound (453 g) fresh or frozen strawberries, thawed
1½ ounces or 7 tablespoons (42 g) confectioners' sugar

For strawberry *pâte de fruit*:
5 ounces or 9 tablespoons (140 g) strawberry purée
4¼ ounces or full ½ cup (119 g) granulated sugar
½ ounce or 2 tablespoons (14 g) g pectin

For balsamic ganache:
3 ounces (84 g) 31 percent white chocolate, chopped
2¼ ounces (63 g) 38 percent milk chocolate, chopped
1¼ ounces or 2½ tablespoons (35 g) heavy cream

¼ ounce or 1 teaspoon (7 g) light corn syrup
1¾ ounces or ¼ cup (49 g) good-quality balsamic vinegar
½ ounce or 1 tablespoon (14 g) granulated sugar
¼ ounce (7 g) cocoa butter, melted and cooled to 90°F (32°C)
¼ ounce or 1½ teaspoons (7 g) salted butter, cubed, soft but not melted

For the foot:
5¼ ounces (147 g) 64 percent bittersweet chocolate, melted

To dip and decorate chocolates:
2 pounds (906 g) 64 percent bittersweet chocolate, tempered

---

1. To make the strawberry purée: Combine the strawberries and sugar in a food processor. Process the fruit on a low speed until completely liquid. Strain through a fine-mesh sieve into a clean bowl. Cover with plastic wrap and keep refrigerated until ready to use.

2. To make the strawberry *pâte de fruit:*
Place the purée and half of the sugar in a small, heavy-bottomed saucepan. Whisk together the other half of the sugar with the g pectin. Heat the purée mixture over medium heat while whisking vigorously. Once the mixture comes to a boil, whisk in the g pectin mixture. Continue to whisk, allowing mixture to come to a second boil. Whisk for 2 minutes more and remove from heat. Pour directly into the prepared pan (see page 128). Shake the pan to spread the *pâte de fruit* into all the crevices. Chill for 20 minutes in the refrigerator. After 20 minutes, let the pan sit at room temperature.

3. To make the ganache: Place the chocolate in a medium-size bowl and set aside. Combine the heavy cream, corn syrup, balsamic vinegar, and sugar in a small, heavy-bottomed saucepan and cook over medium-high heat. Stir until the mixture comes to a full boil. Immediately pour onto the chopped chocolate. Let sit for 2 minutes and then stir to combine. Using a candy thermometer placed in the center of the bowl, check the temperature. Once the ganache has reached 95°F (35°C), stir in the cocoa butter and butter.

Immediately pour directly over the strawberry pâte de fruit layer. Spread evenly using a small offset spatula, knocking the pan if necessary to release any trapped air bubbles. Place the ganache in the freezer for 1 hour. Once the ganache is firm, remove from the freezer.

4. To add the foot: Remove the ganache from the pan by picking up both sides of the plastic wrap. Gently transfer the ganache onto a baking sheet covered with a clean sheet of parchment paper so the ganache is still on top. Heat the foot chocolate in the microwave on 50 percent power for 20 seconds at a time, until it is completely melted. To create a foot, spread a thin layer of the melted chocolate over the chocolate ganache using a small offset spatula. Place in the freezer for 1 hour to set.

5. To cut the filling: Remove the ganache from the freezer and gently flip onto a parchment paper-lined cutting board so the foot is face down. Gently peel off the plastic wrap. Using a sharp, nonserrated knife, trim all four edges. Use a ruler to mark the ganache on all four sides at 1" (2.5 cm) intervals. Match up the notches and cut into squares. Separate the squares onto parchment paper. Allow the squares to sit overnight at room temperature to dry.

6. To dip and decorate the chocolates: To dip, see page 131. Decorate as desired.

PEPPERED PINEAPPLE

My friend Ann best described this combination as follows: "It's just so unexpected. You get the wonderful sweet pineapple taste mixed in with the creaminess of the chocolate. And then all of a sudden there is this sharpness from the pepper that makes you appreciate the pineapple all the more." Given that she's eaten a pound in one sitting, she knows what she's talking about!

DIFFICULT **Yield: 42 chocolates**

For pineapple purée:
1 pound (453 g) fresh pineapple, cubed
1½ ounces or 7 tablespoons (42 g) confectioners' sugar

For pineapple *pâte de fruit:*
5 ounces or 9 tablespoons (140 g) pineapple purée
4¼ ounces or full ½ cup (119 g) granulated sugar
½ ounce or 2 tablespoons (14 g) g pectin

For pineapple ganache:
5¼ ounces (147 g) 38 percent milk chocolate, chopped
¾ ounce (21 g) 64 percent bittersweet chocolate, chopped

2 ounces or ¼ cup (56 g) heavy cream
1 ounce or 3 tablespoons (28 g) pineapple purée
¼ ounce or 1 teaspoon (7 g) light corn syrup
¼ ounce or 1½ teaspoon (7 g) salted butter, cubed, soft but not melted
¼ ounce or full 1 tablespoon (7 g) good-quality dark rum, such as Myers

For the foot:
5¼ ounces (147 g) 38 percent milk chocolate, melted

To dip and decorate chocolates:
2 pounds (906 g) 38 percent milk chocolate, tempered
Freshly ground black pepper to taste

---

1. To make the pineapple purée: Combine the pineapple and sugar in a food processor. Process the fruit on a low speed until completely liquid. Strain through a fine-mesh sieve into a clean bowl. Cover with plastic wrap and keep refrigerated until ready to use.

2. To make the pineapple *pâte de fruit:*
Place the purée and half of the sugar in a small, heavy-bottomed saucepan. In a separate bowl, whisk together the other half of the sugar with the g pectin. Heat the purée mixture over medium heat while whisking vigorously. Once the mix-

ture comes to a boil, whisk in the g pectin mixture. Continue to whisk, allowing mixture to come to a second boil. Whisk for 2 minutes more and remove from heat. Pour directly into the prepared baking pan (see page 128). Shake the pan to spread the *pâte de fruit* into all the crevices. Chill for 20 minutes in the refrigerator. After 20 minutes, let the pan sit at room temperature.

3. To make the ganache: Place the chopped chocolate in a medium-size bowl and set aside. Combine the heavy cream, pineapple purée, and corn syrup in a small, heavy-bottomed saucepan and cook over medium-high heat. Stir until the mixture comes to a full boil. Immediately pour onto the chocolate. Let sit for 2 minutes and then stir to combine. Using a candy thermometer placed in the center of the bowl, check the temperature. Once the ganache has reached 95°F (35°C), stir in the butter and rum. Immediately pour directly over the pineapple pâte de fruit layer. Spread evenly using a small offset spatula, knocking the pan if necessary to release any trapped air bubbles. Place the ganache in the freezer for 1 hour. Once the ganache is firm, remove from the freezer.

4. To add the foot: Remove the ganache from the pan by picking up both sides of the plastic wrap. Gently transfer the ganache onto a baking sheet covered with a clean sheet of parchment paper so the ganache is still on top. Heat the foot chocolate in the microwave on 50 percent power for 20 seconds at a time, until it is completely melted. To create a foot, spread a thin layer of the melted chocolate over the chocolate ganache using a small offset spatula. Place in the freezer for 1 hour.

5. To cut the filling: Remove the ganache from the freezer and gently flip onto a parchment paper-lined cutting board so the foot is face down. Gently peel off plastic wrap. Using a sharp, nonserrated knife, trim all four edges. Use a ruler to mark the ganache on all four sides at 1" (2.5 cm) intervals. Match up the notches and cut the pieces into squares. Separate the squares onto parchment paper. Allow the squares to sit overnight at room temperature to dry.

6. To dip and decorate the chocolates: To dip, see page 131. To decorate, sprinkle with the freshly ground black pepper. Repeat the dipping and decorating process with the remaining squares.

Chapter Eight

Fun Chocolate Confections

This chapter represents some of the best-selling chocolates in my store that happen to also be my favorites to both make and eat. For the most part, these recipes are easier than those in chapters five, six, and seven. Yet they still contain some great techniques that are worth mastering. The lollipop recipe shows you how to create a shape without needing a mold, and the tablet recipes are great examples of how to mold solid pieces. The crispy crunchies show how easy it is to combine basic ingredients to create a fun confection, whereas the popcorn recipe illustrates basic caramel making skills. And if you like the idea of the turtle tablet, use the same concept of a filled candy bar and create your own filled tablet using a filling recipe from chapter six.

Some of the recipes in this chapter require special equipment, such as a tablet mold to make the fruit and nut tablets and the turtle tablets. For the majority of these recipes, however, most of what you will need you probably already own. As when making any other recipes in this book, be sure to have all the components of the recipe ready before you start and read the recipe through before you begin, to be sure you understand it completely.

Right: Rocky Rhode Island Candy Bar, page 164

Chocolate Shotts™ Cookies

I created this recipe when I needed a cookie that had a great chocolate flavor, was not too sweet, was moist and rich on the inside, and stayed slightly crispy on the outside when baked. Whenever we make batches of these in the kitchen we always make more than needed to fill an order, as half of them are eaten by my staff.

Here's a great variation to this recipe: Instead of baking the dough as individual cookies, form the dough into a 1" (2.5 cm)-diameter rope and flatten it out into a rectangle. Bake and cool as directed. Then use the baked log as the bottom of a banana split or any other ice-cream sundae.

EASY   **Yield: 36 1-ounce (28 g) cookies**

For coffee paste:
¼ ounce or full 1 tablespoon (7 g) freshly ground coffee, preferably Italian
3 ounces or 6 tablespoons (84 g) water

For cookies:
8 ounces (224 g) 64 percent bittersweet chocolate, chopped
8 ounces (224 g) 84 percent extra-bittersweet chocolate, chopped
2 ounces or ¼ cup (56 g) salted butter, cubed, room temperature

12 ounces or 1½ cups (336 g) granulated sugar
4 large eggs
⅛ ounce or 1 teaspoon (3.5 g) coffee paste
⅛ ounce or 1 teaspoon (3.5 g) vanilla extract
2 ounces or ½ cup plus 1½ tablespoons (56 g) pastry or cake flour
⅛ ounce or 1 teaspoon (3.5 g) baking powder
Pinch salt
14¼ ounces (400 g) semisweet chocolate chips
4 ounces (112 g) pecans, shelled, toasted, chopped

---

1. To make the coffee paste: Place the ground coffee in a small bowl. Bring the water to a rapid boil, pour over the coffee, and stir to dissolve the coffee grounds. Set aside until ready to use. This will make more than the required amount. The remaining paste can be stored in the refrigerator in an airtight container, but must be stirred thoroughly before each use.

2. To make cookies: Lightly butter a large baking sheet and set aside until ready to use. Combine chocolates and melt over a double boiler. Set aside. In the bowl of an electric mixer

fitted with the paddle attachment, mix together the butter and sugar on low. The mixture will still look loose and grainy. Slowly add the eggs, one at a time, scraping the sides of the bowl and mixing well between additions. Add the coffee and vanilla extract, and mix well. Scrape the sides of the bowl. Sift together the flour, baking powder, and the salt. Slowly add the dry ingredients to the mixing bowl. Mix on low until everything is incorporated. Slowly drizzle the melted chocolate into the cookie dough while mixing. Continue to mix on low speed until everything is incorporated. Scrape the sides of the bowl. Add the chocolate chips and the pecans, and mix just until combined. Remove from the mixer.

3. To bake: Preheat the oven to 350°F (180°C). Using a 1-ounce (20 g) ice cream scoop or two tablespoons, place portions of dough on a parchment paper-lined baking sheet, spacing each cookie 2" (5 cm) apart. Bake for 10 to 12 minutes; the center of the cookies should still be slightly soft. Remove from oven and allow the cookies to sit on the baking sheet for an additional 3 minutes. Then transfer the cookies to a wire rack to cool.

4. To store: Cookies will keep at room temperature, stored in an airtight container, for seven days. Unbaked cookie dough can be frozen for up to three months if well wrapped in plastic wrap and placed in a freezer storage bag.

DRINKING CHOCOLATE

Hot chocolate is a hot commodity these days. This recipe will show you how to create your own hot chocolate powder for a delicious warm drink. My staff calls this a "liquid brownie" because it is so rich and satisfying.

This recipe can also be easily adapted into a cold beverage. Simply make the powder and then the warm drink according to the recipe. Then allow the chocolate to cool down in the refrigerator. Adding Kahlúa and vodka and shaking it over ice makes for a very tasty chocolate martini!

EASY **Powder Yield: 13¼ ounces** or **2¼ cups (371 g)**

Liquid Yield: 9 ounces or **1 cup (252 g)**

For drinking chocolate powder:
8¼ ounces (231 g) 64 percent bittersweet chocolate, chopped
1 ounce or ⅓ cup (28 g) nonfat dry milk
4 ounces or 1 cup (112 g) Guittard sweet ground chocolate

For liquid drinking chocolate:
1½ ounces or ¼ cup (42 g) drinking chocolate powder
8 ounces or 1 cup (224 g) whole milk

---

1. To make drinking chocolate powder:
Combine the dark chocolate and the nonfat dry milk in a food processor. Grind on a low speed until the chocolate forms small granules. Scrape the sides of bowl and under the blade with a rubber spatula. Make sure the chocolate does not get too hot, or it will melt. If the chocolate begins to soften while in the food processor, let it cool for 5 to 10 minutes. Once the chocolate is a fine powder, add the sweet ground powder. Process for 10 to 20 seconds, or until completely incorporated. Store in an airtight container at 60°F to 65°F (16°C to 18°C) for no longer than six months.

2. To make liquid drinking chocolate: Combine the chocolate powder and the milk in a small, heavy-bottomed saucepan. Cook over medium heat, stirring constantly with a whisk. Once all the powder has completely dissolved and it reaches a rapid boil, remove from heat and serve.

CHOCOLATE LOLLIPOPS

Everyone loves lollipops, and these are fun to make for kids and adults alike. This is a basic recipe that can be adapted myriad ways. Here I have used dark chocolate but milk or white work just as well. Likewise, while this recipe calls for orange oil, any flavor natural oil will work.

This is a recipe for handmade lollipops. Molded versions are just as easy if you can find lollipop molds at a candy-making supply store where you can also buy lollipop sticks. To make molded lollipops, simply place the lollipop sticks in their correct place in the mold and fill the mold with tempered chocolate.

EASY   **Yield: 10 lollipops**

4 ounces (112 g) 64 percent bittersweet chocolate, tempered

2 drops orange oil

---

1. To mold: Line a baking sheet with a clean piece of parchment or waxed paper. Place lollipop sticks in a line lengthwise across the baking sheet, spaced 3" (3.5 cm) apart. Combine the tempered dark chocolate and orange oil, and stir well. Use a pastry bag, or make your own using a large sandwich bag. Pour the flavored chocolate into the bag and push it all down into one of the corners. Then cut an opening out of the corner of the bag. Starting at the tip of the lollipop stick, pipe in a circular motion, left to right on the parchment paper, connecting each circle, and making smaller circles as you pipe inward. Repeat this process nine more times for each of the other lollipops.

2. To set: Place in the refrigerator for 5 minutes, or until the lollipops have set. Remove from the refrigerator and let the lollipops sit at room temperature for 15 minutes. Gently lift the lollipops off the parchment paper. If they do not release easily, allow them to sit for a few extra minutes to finish setting.

Fruit and Nut Tablets

This is my version of chocolate bark. I prefer to make it in molded tablet form for a more elegant look. Packaged together in a bundle and tied with a pretty ribbon, these make a great gift that is both elegant and delicious.

I like to use assorted candied fruit and nuts when I make this recipe. If you have a favorite trail mix or prefer other topping combinations, those will work just as well. The general idea is to choose toppings with a variety of textures and flavors, for a fully dimensional experience. Use enough topping on each tablet to cover enough of the chocolate but not so much that the chocolate flavor is lost. As always, keep a good balance.

This recipe calls for a three-cavity tablet mold. Remember to wash the mold in warm, soapy water and rinse well. Always dry with a soft cloth and polish the mold cavities gently with a cotton ball before using. Keep in mind that any scratches to the inside surface of the mold cavities will show up on the finished tablets.

EASY

DARK   **Yield: 3 tablets**
9 ounces (252 g) 64 percent bittersweet chocolate, tempered
21 whole almonds, toasted
30 candied orange pieces
45 golden raisins, tossed in granulated sugar

MILK   **Yield: 3 tablets**
9 ounces (252 g) 38 percent milk chocolate, tempered

21 whole hazelnuts, toasted
30 candied ginger pieces
45 golden raisins, tossed in granulated sugar

WHITE   **Yield: 3 tablets**
9 ounces (252 g) 29 percent white chocolate, tempered
21 whole pistachios, shelled, lightly toasted
30 dried cranberries, tossed in granulated sugar
45 golden raisins, tossed in granulated sugar

---

1. To mold: Ladle 3 ounces of tempered chocolate into each tablet mold—in total, 9 ounces of chocolate. Completely fill each mold with chocolate. Use the blade of a chef's knife or offset spatula to remove any excess chocolate from the top of the mold. Immediately cover each bar with the dried fruit and nuts.

2. To set: Place in the refrigerator for 15 minutes. You should begin to see the sides of the bars releasing from the sides of the mold. Remove from the refrigerator and allow to sit at room temperature for 15 minutes. Gently invert mold over clean work surface and tap lightly to release tablets.

CRISPY CRUNCHIES

My staff calls these tempting little treats "poppers" because they are so tasty and easy to eat. I call them crispy crunchies because of their texture. Made with granulated almonds, pistachios, candied orange peel, and crispy rice cereal, they are a great balance of salty, sweet, chewy, and crunchy.

This version is made with white chocolate, which allows the flavor of the candied orange to shine through. However, they are equally as delicious when made with milk or dark chocolate, either of which can be substituted for the white chocolate in equal amounts.

EASY   **Yield: 35 pieces**

9 ounces (252 g) 29 percent white chocolate, tempered

¾ ounce (21 g) cocoa butter, tempered

7 ounces (196 g) almonds, toasted, finely chopped

1¾ ounces (49 g) pistachios, shelled, finely chopped

3½ ounces (98 g) candied orange peel, chopped

¾ ounce or scant 1 cup (21 g) puffed rice cereal

---

1. Combine the tempered white chocolate and tempered cocoa butter. Combine all the dry ingredients and fold in tempered chocolate mixture. Use a small ice-cream scoop or two table- spoons to drop loose scoops onto a clean sheet of parchment paper. Allow to set for twenty minutes.

CHOCOLATE-COVERED CARAMEL POPCORN

This is a hands-down best-seller in our store. And when we make it in the kitchen, it is way too tempting to walk past without grabbing a handful. I mean, what could be better? Fresh, salty popcorn and crunchy nuts covered in creamy caramel and then drizzled with chocolate! This is a crowd-pleaser for any age.

Here are a couple of tips when making this recipe. One: Use one "pop and serve" bag when popping popcorn. It's quick and easy and eliminates part of the mess. Remember to use plain-flavored popcorn. Two: This recipe works better in less humid environments and seasons. The popcorn will stay crunchy longer when kept away from moisture. If you make this recipe on a warm, humid summer day, prepare it just before serving. In cool, dry winter weather, this recipe can be made several days in advance if stored in an airtight container.

A fun variation is to create popcorn lollipops. Simply shape the warm popcorn into a disk or tube and insert a lollipop stick.

EASY   **Yield: 1 pound popcorn**

1 ounce or 2 tablespoons (28 g) water

2 ounces or ¼ cup (56 g) granulated sugar

1 ounce or 8 teaspoons (28 g) brown sugar

¾ ounce or 1 tablespoon (21 g) light corn syrup

½ ounce or 1 tablespoon (14 g) salted butter

1¾ ounces (49 g) Spanish peanuts, skin removed

Pinch kosher salt

Pinch baking soda

2¼ ounces or 5 cups (63 g) popped popcorn

8½ ounces (238 g) 64 percent bittersweet chocolate, tempered

---

1. To mix: Combine the water, sugars, corn syrup, butter, and peanuts in a large, heavy-bottomed saucepan. Cook over high heat, stirring continuously, until the mixture begins to thicken, and reaches a medium amber color (250°F [121°C]). Remove from heat and add the salt and baking soda. Stir well. Add the popcorn, stir quickly, and immediately pour onto a nonstick, flat surface. Be careful: the caramel will be very hot. Use the back of a nonstick cookie sheet to flatten out the popcorn to a ¾" to 1" (1.9 to 2.5 cm) thickness. Let the popcorn cool.

2. To decorate: Pour the tempered dark chocolate into a pastry bag or large sandwich bag, and cut a hole in a corner for an opening. Pipe stripes back and forth across the cooled popcorn. Once the chocolate has set, use a spatula to break it apart and off the nonstick surface.

ROCKY RHODE ISLAND CANDY BAR

This recipe is a twist on the classic rocky road flavor combination. I like it because of its strong peanut butter flavor and the variety of textures.

EASY **Yield: 16 candy bars**

For peanut butter ganache:
9¹⁄₂ ounces or 1 cup plus 2 tablespoons (271 g) creamy peanut butter
4³⁄₄ ounces (133 g) 38 percent milk chocolate, melted and cooled to 88°F
1¹⁄₄ ounces (35 g) cocoa butter, melted and cooled to 90°F (32°C)
Pinch kosher salt

For graham cracker layer:
1¹⁄₄ ounces or ¹⁄₃ cup (35 g) peanut butter ganache
1¹⁄₄ ounces or ¹⁄₃ cup (35 g) graham cracker crumbs

For peanut butter–marshmallow layer:
7 ounces or 4¹⁄₄ cups (196 g) miniature marshmallows
7³⁄₄ ounces (217 g) Spanish peanuts, skin removed, toasted

For the foot:
5¹⁄₄ ounces (147 g) 64 percent bittersweet chocolate, melted

To finish the candy bar:
3 ounces (84 g) 64 percent bittersweet chocolate, tempered

1. To make the ganache: Combine the peanut butter and the melted milk chocolate. Stir in the melted cocoa butter and salt.

2. To make the graham cracker layer: [A]. Measure out 1¹⁄₄ ounces or ¹⁄₃ cup (35 g) of peanut butter ganache and mix with the graham cracker crumbs **[B]**. Stir well. Pour into the prepared pan (see page 128) **[C]**, and spread evenly using a small offset spatula **[D]**, knocking the pan if necessary to release any trapped air bubbles. Set aside while you prepare the next layer.

3. To make the peanut butter–marshmallow layer: Combine the remaining peanut butter ganache, marshmallows **[E]**, and approximately half of the peanuts **[F]**. Stir until all ingredients are incorporated **[G]**. Pour directly over the graham cracker layer **[H]**. Smooth out, lightly pushing down with a spatula to remove any trapped air bubbles. Sprinkle the remaining peanuts on top **[I]**, and lightly press down to secure the peanuts. Place the pan in the refrigerator for 30 minutes to set. Then remove from the refrigerator and let it sit at room temperature for 30 minutes.

4. To add the foot: Remove the candy slab from the pan by picking up both sides of the plastic wrap. Gently flip the candy slab over onto a baking sheet covered with a clean piece of plastic wrap or sheet of parchment paper so the graham cracker layer is now bottom side up. Peel the plastic off the bottom of the layer. Heat the foot chocolate in the microwave on 50 percent power for 20 seconds at a time, until it is completely melted. To create a foot, spread a thin layer of the melted chocolate over the graham cracker layer using a small offset spatula. Place in the freezer for 30 minutes to set.

5. To cut into pieces: Remove candy bar from the freezer and gently flip onto a parchment paper-lined cutting board so the foot is face down. Let candy bar sit at room temperature for 30 minutes before using a sharp, nonserrated knife to trim all four edges. Next, cut the large square in half down the middle. Separate the

two halves and cut each into 1" × ¾" (2.5 × 1.8 cm) long bars. Place the bars on a clean sheet of parchment paper.

6. To finish: Place the tempered dark chocolate in a pastry bag or large sandwich bag with the tip cut off on one corner for an opening. Pipe chocolate stripes across the top of each candy bar. You can also use a fork or spoon to drizzle the chocolate across the candy bars, if you prefer. Allow the chocolate to fully set.

Turtle Tablets

These delicious candy bars are a variation on the American classic known as turtles. Created for a more sophisticated consumer, they are a perfect balance of dark chocolate and creamy caramel. The candied pecans add a nice textural contrast as well as another flavor dimension. I would be remiss, however, if I did not add a warning to this recipe: if you make them and give them out as gifts, expect to get repeated requests for more!

EASY **Yield: 6 tablets**

For caramel filling:
2 ounces or ¼ cup (56 g) granulated sugar
4¼ ounces or full ½ cup (119 g) heavy cream, warmed
Pinch kosher salt
10 ounces (280 g) 29 percent white chocolate, melted
½ ounce or 1 tablespoon (14 g) salted butter, cubed, soft but not melted

For candied pecans:
1 ounce or 1 tablespoon plus 1 teaspoon (28 g) light corn syrup
5 ounces (140 g) whole pecans, shelled

For chocolate shells:
1½ pounds (672 g) 72 percent extra bittersweet chocolate, tempered

1. To make the caramel filling: Place the sugar and a small amount of water (enough to make it the consistency of wet sand) in a heavy-bottomed saucepan and cook over medium-high heat. Cook until medium to dark amber in color. Slowly and carefully add the warm heavy cream and salt. Remove from heat; mix until well combined and smooth in consistency. Pour the mixture over the melted white chocolate and let sit for 1 minute. Stir until combined, then add the butter and mix until smooth and homogenous. Cool to room temperature.

2. To make the candied pecans: Preheat oven to 325°F (170°C). Place the corn syrup in a small, heavy-bottomed saucepan and cook over medium-high heat, until it becomes warm and thinner in consistency. Pour the syrup over

the pecans and carefully toss until the nuts are fully coated. Spread the nuts on a parchment paper-lined baking sheet and bake in the preheated oven for 15 minutes. Cool and set aside for later use.

3. To assemble the tablets: Use a large ladle to completely fill all the cavities in the tablet mold with the tempered chocolate. Hold the mold upside down over the bowl of tempered chocolate and tap the side with the back of a chef's knife to allow any excess chocolate to drip out. Place the mold upside down on a parchment paper–lined baking sheet and let sit for a couple of minutes to remove any remaining excess chocolate. (You only want a thin coating to remain in the mold to create the shell of the tablet.) After a few minutes, when the chocolate just begins to set, scrape the top of each tablet cavity with an offset spatula or chef's knife to make a clean edge. Allow the chocolate shell to completely set.

4. To fill the chocolate shells: Place caramel filling into a piping bag or large sandwich bag, cut a small opening, and fill each tablet cavity to about ⅛" (3 mm) from the top of the mold. Leave enough space to cover the mold with chocolate at the end. Place the mold in the refrigerator for about 20 minutes to allow the filling to set, then ladle about 8 ounces or 1 cup

(224 g) of tempered chocolate over the filled tablet cavities; use more or less as needed to completely cover the caramel filling.

5. To finish: Spread the chocolate evenly over the top of the mold using a large offset spatula, removing excess chocolate. Sprinkle the candied pecans on the wet chocolate. Return the mold to the refrigerator for at least 30 minutes. Remove from the refrigerator and invert gently onto a clean surface, tapping the mold if necessary to release the tablets.

How to Mold Chocolate

The following molds are filled with caramel and topped with candied pecans for Turtle Tablets, but follow the same process for any of the book's molded chocolate recipes.

1. Fill the cavities in the tablet mold with tempered chocolate.

2. Hold the mold upside down and tap the side with the back of a chef's knife to allow any excess chocolate to drip out.

3. Scrape the top of each tablet cavity with an offset spatula or knife to create a clean edge.

4. Using a piping bag, fill each tablet cavity with the caramel filling, stopping about ⅛" (3 mm) from the top of the mold and allow filling to set.

5. Once you have covered the caramel with a layer of tempered chocolate, use an offset spatula or chef's knife to smooth away any excess chocolate.

6. Add the candied pecans before the chocolate has completely hardened.

SOURCES

This is by no means a complete source list. Here are just a few places you will find items needed to make the recipes in this book. For questions or comments about the recipes and techniques in this book, email book@garrisonconfections.com.

Bakeware and Assorted Pastry Supplies

Bed Bath & Beyond
bedbathandbeyond.com

Kerekes
6103 15th Avenue
Brooklyn, NY 11219
Phone: (718) 232-7044/
(800) 525-5556
Fax: (718) 232-4416
www.bakedeco.com

N.Y. Cake and Baking Distributor
56 West 22nd Street
New York, NY 10010
Phone: (212) 675-2253/
(800) 942-2539
Fax: (212) 675-7099
www.nycake.com

Sur La Table
www.surlatable.com

Williams-Sonoma
www.williamsonoma.com

Wilton Industries
2240 West 75th Street
Woodridge, IL 60517
Phone: (630) 963-1818/
(800) 794-5866
Fax: (630) 963-7196/
(888) 824-9520
E-mail: info@wilton.com
www.wilton.com

Infused Oils and Flavorings

Amoretti
451 S. Lombard Street
Oxnard, CA 93030
Phone: (818) 718-1239/
(800) 266-7388
Fax: (818) 718-0204
www.amoretti.com

Boyajian Incorporated
144 Will Drive
Canton, MA 02021
Phone: (781) 828-9966/
(800) 965-0665
Fax: (781) 828-9922
E-mail: customerservice@
boyajianinc.com
www.boyajianinc.com

Molds and Other Professional Supplies

Chef Rubber
Phone: (702) 614-9350
www.chefrubber.com

Garrison Confections, Inc.
815 Hope Street
Providence, RI 02906
Phone: (401) 490-2740
Fax: (401) 490-2742
www.garrisonconfections.com

J. B. Prince Company
36 East 31st Street
New York, NY 10016
Phone: (800) 473-0577
Fax: (212) 683-4488
www.jbprince.com

Tomric Systems—MOLDS
85 River Rock Drive #202
Buffalo, NY 14207
Phone: (716) 854-6050
Fax: (716) 854-7363
www.tomric.com

Chocolate

Guittard Chocolate Company
10 Guittard Road
Burlingame, CA 94010
Phone: (650) 697-4427/
(800) 468-2462
Fax: (650) 692-2761
www.guittard.com

Gourmail
Phone: (800) 366-5900 Ext. 96
Fax: (508) 752-6645
www.gourmail.com

www.chocolatebysparrow.com

www.chocolateman.net

www.chocolatesource.com

ACKNOWLEDGMENTS

Many people helped create this book, and I would be remiss if I did not give them credit:

- My wife, Tina Wright, for taking my ideas and putting them into words
- Kara Leo, my production manager, for keeping my kitchen running smoothly so I could concentrate on this project
- Kendra Mellar, for her patience in testing all these recipes as many times as necessary
- Madeline Polss, for her infinite patience, her creativity, and, most important, her fabulous sense of photography—"click, click."
- Candice Janco, for choosing me for this project, and the folks at Quarry Books, for backing her decision
- Tomric Systems, for generously donating all the chocolate and candy molds used in these recipes
- Ann Martini, for her endless editing advice

Throughout my career I have been fortunate to work with many talented professionals whom I would like to thank:

- Matt Ries, a chef who made me *really* think about food
- Jacques Torres, for making time for me on that cold day in December 1993
- Chef Jean Jacques Rachou, for letting me shine
- Pascal Caffet, for the opportunity
- Stephane Glacier, who taught me what hot really means
- Jay Priest, who always made it happen
- Richard Capizzi, for believing in Garrison Confections years before it became a company and for helping me get it off the ground when it finally did
- Dorian O'Connell, who made the move to Providence a successful one
- Jeffrey Dryfoos, or I will never hear the end of it

There are many more people who helped me get to where I am today and I could fill pages with their names. You all know who you are and how grateful I am for your support.

Finally, I would like to thank my mother-in-law, Erika, without whom Garrison Confections may never have happened.

About the Author

Andrew Shotts is the owner of Garrison Confections, a Providence, Rhode Island-based artisanal chocolate company, known for its seasonal collections. A graduate of the Culinary Institute of America, Andrew discovered his passion for chocolate early on in his culinary career, when he began experimenting with desserts and chocolates that incorporated the freshest hand-picked ingredients, and developed a deep commitment to seasonality that is the foundation of Garrison Confections.

Andrew has showcased his talents as executive pastry chef at La Côte Basque and the Russian Tea Room in New York City. He was the corporate pastry chef for the San Francisco-based Guittard Chocolate Company, where he helped develop and launch the E. Guittard line of high-end couverture chocolate. He has been named one of *Pastry Art & Design's* "Ten Best Pastry Chefs in America" in both 2000 and 2002, and was recognized as a "Top Ten Artisanal Chocolatier" by *USA Today*. He is the winner of the silver medal at both the 2000 and 2001 National Pastry Team Championships, and in 2005 represented the United States at the largest international pastry competition in the world, the 2005 World Pastry Cup, in France, bringing home the bronze medal.

Andrew can be seen frequently on the Food Network, and has graced the pages of many national food and travel magazines.

About the Photographer

Madeline Polss, a uniquely talented food and lifestyle photographer, has contributed to many cookbooks and magazines such as *Gourmet, Food Arts, Modern Bride, Art Culinaire, Parenting, American Way*, and *Wine Spectator*.

Also an avid cook, she began attracting food clients early in her career, and quickly developed techniques that set her work apart. Madeline's passion for food and lifestyle photography and enthusiasm for travel has made her widely sought after by clients who are interested in her distinctive style.

Having worked for many years in Philadelphia, New York, and Houston, Madeline now lives in Newport, Rhode Island, where she continues to shoot assignment and stock images, both on location and in her newly constructed studio. More of her work can be seen at www.mpolssphoto.com.

INDEX